Related Events to the Second Coming of the Christ

CORONATION OF THE CHRIST

&

THE MARRIAGE SUPPER

Volume 4

Michael W. Dewar

Copyright © 2023 by Michael W. Dewar
CORONATION OF THE CHRIST & THE MARRIAGE SUPPER OF THE LAMB
Related Events to the Second Coming of the Christ

ISBN: 979-8-9856973-1-5

Published by Dwelling Place Cleansing
Brooklyn, New York 11236
United States of America
DPSCleansing.com

All rights reserved solely by the author. The author guarantees all contents are original and do not infringe upon the legal rights of any other person or work. No part of this book may be reproduced in any form without the permission of the author.

Unless otherwise indicated, Bible quotations are taken
from The Holy Bible, New International Version(NIV).
Copyright © 1973, 1978, 1984 by International Bible
Society; The Holy Bible, King James Version(KJV); and
The Holy Bible, New Living Translation(NLT). Copyright
© 1996 by Tyndale House Publishers, Inc.

Dedication

This book is dedicated to my granddaughter, Lorain, whom I first saw and held August 21st, 2022. May you grow in health, flourish in soul, intellect, and in love of God and neighbor.

"Crown Him with many of crowns the lamb upon His throne."

CONTENTS

Preface..vii
Introduction..9

Part I

Chapter 1 Israel's God, the King Who Reigns............................15
Chapter 2 Understanding Jesus' Kingship and Government....29
Chapter 3 Kingship Imposed and Declined..............................43

Part II

Chapter 4 Exaltation of the Christ..63
Chapter 5 The Coronation of the Christ...................................77

Part III

Chapter 6 The Marriage Supper Celebration...........................91
Chapter 7 The Warrior King Returns to Reign.......................103
End Notes...109
About the Author...111
Other Books by this Author..113

My Kingdom is not of this world"
(John 18:36).

PREFACE

As you have already observed, perhaps, this is Volume 4 in a series of 10, dealing with *Related Events to the Second Coming of the Christ*. One reason for writing is to prod everyday believers into a state of spiritual wakefulness to the present time and what's coming. It is easy to become preoccupied or burnout from the cares of life that we lose sight of what is coming (Matt.13:22). Now and then the Bible nudges us to soberness (1Thes.5:1-9).

Having led congregations for more than forty years now, I am now noticing a kind of boredom, weariness among some believers concerning their spiritual life and things spiritual. It is a lack of readiness toward the coming of the Lord. This spiritual condition is akin to falling asleep before surgery as the anesthetic begins to take effect. The culture can drug us into a type of spiritual dazedness, so that we are not fully asleep and not fully awake.

But we must be fully awake and in a state of readiness to make it in the rapture, and we must have made the rapture to participate in the *Coronation of the Christ* and *The Marriage Supper* because these events will take place in heaven.

This book is not for everyone, it is for the few, like yourself, who already have some spiritual knowledge and wish to position yourself for a more complete *spiritual insight* to inherit the joyous eternity moving toward you. Those without spiritual insight and not awake toward what's coming, may have to settle for the unpleasant destiny that is theirs by default.

Again, this volume and the others in the series disclosed the unfolding of the joyous future that is yours in Christ. Each volume can be read in one sitting. But they are best read slowly and reflectively, not as spiritually microwaved fast-food. Reflective reading is best for spiritual edification, blessing, and nourishment.

Let me say thanks to few of the many people that helped me on my pilgrimage over the years: James Pollard and His wife Regina of Zion Baptist Church in Ardmore, PA., Joseph and Betty Woodson of Media, PA., James and Gladys Austin who served at the Second Baptist Church of Media (while I was pastor there and James as deacon).

This series is written while serving as pastor of the New York Congregational Baptist Church (NYCBC) in Brooklyn, New York. Thanks to the entire body of believers here. We had a joyous time working with each other, serving our blessed Lord. We are destined to enjoy a blessed future with countless millions as revealed in this book and the others in the series.

INTRODUCTION
Offices of the Christ

Jesus has many offices and titles, but the three prominent ones are Prophet, Priest, and King. The fourth office is that of Judge which we tend not to talk about, except now and then we say, He is coming back to judge the living and the dead. The function of Judge is uniquely addressed in Volume 2 and will be addressed again Volume 9 or 10 in the context of the final Judgment.

As believers, we have experienced the Christ in the prophetic role during His earthly ministry. He preached, served as the Master teacher, and brought deliverance to many from sickness, disease, demonic oppression, and even death. Through the shedding of His precious blood, the giving of His life on the cross, He purchased eternal redemption for the human family.

By doing all these things, Jesus perfectly fulfilled the prophetic Scriptures of the Messiah as recorded in the Hebrew Bible. He made that fact clear to His unbelieving hometown synagogue, when He read the following words from the scroll of the Prophet Isaiah about the Messiah:

> The Spirit of the Lord is upon me, because he has anointed me to proclaim good news to the poor. He has sent me to proclaim freedom for the prisoners, and the recovery of sight for the blind, to set the oppressed free, to proclaim the year of the Lord's favor. (Luke 4:17-21)

Note that after He was through reading, He rolled up the scroll and gave it back to the minister, then commented: "Today this scripture is fulfilled in you hearing" (v.21). In other words, I am the Messiah! His hearers were puzzled and said, "Is not this Joseph's son?" In other words, we know this boy, he is the carpenter's son; we know his mother, Mary, and we know His brothers. How can he say, Isaiah's prophesy is about Him?

Isaiah wrote this prophecy 700 years ago. Jesus was brought up in this community of Nazareth! With that they took offense of him and threw him out of their synagogue (vv.29-30). And because of their unbelief, Jesus could do no mighty work in His hometown of Nazareth, so He moved to Capernaum, a fishing village of Galilee (vv.31-32).

Another amazing story in which Jesus asserts that He fulfills the Hebrew Bible, and that all its prophets spoke of Him is seen next. The story unfolds on this wise—after His resurrection, two despondent, heavy-hearted travelers who knew His ministry well were journeying to a village outside of Jerusalem. They were talking about the crucifixion that happened few days before. They were sad because they feared the religious leaders made a blunder in having Jesus of Nazareth crucified. Just about then, a stranger joined them, who happened to be the resurrected Christ in disguised. He asked them why they were so sad?

They said, Sir, are you a stranger in Jerusalem, haven't you heard what has happened, how Jesus of Nazareth whom we supposed was the Messiah was crucified? Besides, this is the third day and some women brought us strange news, that they saw the man alive that was crucified and buried.

The stranger said to them, well the prophets did write that the Messiah would suffer, be killed, buried, and raised again from the dead on the third day. Starting with the writings of Moses, then all the prophets, He explained to them concerning Jesus of Nazareth.

Just about then the travelers reached their destination. They said to the stranger, it is already late, spend the evening with us. The stranger, still in disguised agreed. As they sat at meal, the stranger took bread, gave thanks, broke it, and gave to them—at that point their eyes were opened and they recognized they were talking to Jesus, and He disappeared. They remarked, did not our hearts burn within us as He opened the Scriptures to us. Being overjoyed, they immediately returned to Jerusalem to report to the disciples how they had seen Jesus ((Luke 24:13-35).

Consider the statement—"Starting with Moses, then all the prophets he explained to them concerning Jesus of Nazareth." It signals to us that the Old Testament is the New Testament (NT) concealed, and the New Testament is the Old Testament (OT) revealed. Now you can understand why Jesus declares in the Sermon of the Mount, "Do not think that I am come to abolish the Law or the Prophets, I have not come to abolish them but to fulfill them...until heaven and earth disappear, not the smallest letter, nor the least stroke of a pen, will by any means, disappear from the Law until everything is accomplished" (Matt.5:17-18).

In substance, Jesus is saying He completes the Hebrew Scriptures. The Jews, therefore, will never understand their own Scriptures until they embrace Jesus Christ as the apostle Paul did.

Before his conversion, Saul (Paul) was zealous for God to the point of destroying followers of Christ. He was sincere, but sincerely wrong. Jesus was the missing piece of the puzzle. When he embraced Jesus as the Messiah, Savior and Lord, the eyes of his understanding were opened to the Hebrew Scriptures. The same is true for all the apostles. But sadly, that spiritual blindness still vails national Israel to this day (Rom.9:1-5, 10:1-4).

Paul's encounter with Jesus Christ lifted the vail from his eyes and transformed him for good. Christ completes the Hebrew Scriptures and by extension the New Testament (NT), for the NT is the story about Jesus Christ, the Messiah. The Bible is one continuing story of redemption through Jesus Christ from Genesis to Revelation. It is a story about the Jewish Messiah who is the Savior of all humankind.

Jesus Christ embodies the prophetic ministry of the Hebrew Bible (the OT), and He embodies the Old Testament priesthood, judgeship, and kingship. That is why we say, Jesus is Prophet, Priest, King, and this book adds a fourth office, that of Judge.

The Bible teaches that the ascended Jesus Christ now serves in the sanctuary in heaven as the Mediatorial High Priest over His Church (Heb.4:14-16; Eph.4:8-13; 1John 2:1-2). Believers are serving in the earthly sanctuary as priests and under-shepherds with the guidance and empowerment of the blessed Holy Spirit (Acts 20:28; 1Peter 2:9, 5:2-4; Rev. 2-3).

We learn from the Word of God that Jesus is also serving as Judge now over His Church, a function that is less popular in pulpits and theological writings. This function as Judge over His people is not in a *punitive* sense but *corrective*, to discipline (Heb.12:3-11; Rev.2-3).[1]

By extension His role as Judge also affects unbelievers who are excessively, and persistently wicked and oppressive to people. In addition to God's common grace, the risen, ascended, and exalted Christ is now working through the blessed Holy Spirit with acts of *conviction*, *discomfort*, and *suffering* to prod unbelievers to repentance (John 16:7-10).

If that does not work, He removes them by the judgment of human law, physical incapacitation, or death (Gen.6:1-8,19:24; Rom.13:1-5). Sometimes death comes through natural disasters, for God is providentially at work in the world (Matt.6:25-34).

We Christians tend to think God is only at work in the Church, but that is mistaken thinking. God's love is for the whole world; His Son is given for the redemption of all humankind (John 3:16). And the Holy Spirit, though resident in the Church, also has a mission to the unregenerate world and that includes conviction, leading to salvation, and to administer judgment (John 16:7-11). Otherwise, if God is not judging people now, the coming Judgment could not be final. Final implies previous judgments. Jesus' full role as Judge will be unveiled at the Final Judgment.

In the Old Testament, God the Father, the God of Israel, is frequently addressed as LORD or King. In the Psalm and Isaiah, God is depicted as the King who reigns (Ps.97:1, 99:1; Isa.6:1-13). The New Testament reveals God as Father (Matt.6:1-9,14-17).

In as much as we accorded the title of King to Jesus Christ, He did not assume or meet the Jewish expectation or fully accepted or rejected the title from any creature during His first advent. But we know He came into this world as King and will return to earth under the full embrace of the titles, KING of Kings, LORD of Lords (Rev.19:16). In His first advent, Jesus frequently referred to Himself as the Son of Man but not as King. Yet, He never rejected the title either, but He strongly resisted and objected to anyone crowning Him King. Attempts were made to crown Him king.

This book explores this issue of Jesus as King, why He refused the role of King while He was upon earth, His heavenly coronation, and full acceptance of the title and role of King. We will also discuss who does the crowning, who else is crowned with Him, His reign, and His Kingdom. I assert that by understanding the coronation and Kingship of the Christ, we stand in a better position to understand His eternal reign and Kingdom and our role as redeemed human beings in that kingdom.

CHAPTER 1

ISRAEL'S GOD, THE KING WHO REIGNS

Overview

From the first century A.D. to date, Christians have been waiting with eager expectation for the return of the Christ, not just as an ordinary king, but as KING of Kings and LORD of Lords (Rev.19:16). But from whence these royal titles of nobility?

Did ambitious followers Christ invent and attach them to Jesus Christ to make Him look great and play the part they created? Or perhaps, we are witnessing the true unfolding drama created by God Himself? I am convinced, we are witnessing a divine drama started not in the peasant village of Nazareth where Jesus grew up, but in eternity past and is unfolding to eternity future. It is a mysterious drama, started with God in Christ, and will end with God in Christ. The writer of the epistle to the Hebrews speaks of Jesus as the "author and finisher of our faith" (Heb.12:1-2 KJV).

Our concern in this book is the lead title, KING of Kings, LORD of Lords conferred upon the Christ under which He returns to reign (Rev. 19: 16). How did Jesus He acquire these royal titles of leadership?

Born in Bethlehem and grew up in the peasant village of Nazareth as the son of a carpenter, Jesus did not travel far from that locality, not even to Rome. He did not rise to any high religious or political office. He was an itinerant preacher and healer who gained popularity with the common folks but at the irritation of the religious elite of His own kin folks. This animosity festered into the conspiracy leading to His death. These are the facts of simple, common history.

But from a spiritual perspective, the events of Christ's death and resurrection are much more complex than simple or common history. It is a divine drama that is still unfolding before us all.

During His earthly ministry, Jesus claimed the titles of Messiah, Son of man, and Son of God. But the religious elite of His people did not consider Him qualified by birth or schooling to assume such titles. In fact, they charged Him with blasphemy for using the title, "Son of God, " and framed him with sedition for not rejecting the title "king of the Jews" (John 19:1-16). The elite class was also jealous of Him because He was popular with the people, and they could not harness that power and influence to do their biddings (Matt.26:1-4, 59-67).

For these, among other things, they pressured the Roman governor to have Jesus executed for His claim of Kingship. They claimed, there is one king and that's Caesar, therefore, if you let this man go, you are not Caesar's friend; that was a threatening, political hand grenade hurled at the Roman governor.

The governor adjusted his attitude and tried Jesus. But the evidence was so overwhelming in Jesus' favor, the governor found Him innocent. But that declaration of innocence greatly infuriated the enemies of Jesus, thus forcing the governor into a conundrum.

The choice was between condemning an innocent man to death and the appearance of being politically right. For political expediency, the governor capitulated, and had Jesus executed to appease the religious elite. This group was headed by the High Priest Caiaphas, also called, the chief priest; he passionately wanted Jesus dead (John 19:1-22).

The four Gospels are four accounts of what happened. The execution of Jesus of Nazareth was a conspiracy of powerful people, a volatile mix of religion and politics. An innocent man died the shameful, excruciating, disgraceful death by crucifixion. Yet, amidst all that human injustice and cruelty, God was redemptively at work. The actors in this drama meant it for evil, but God used it for His own purpose. The darkest day in human history is today called, Good Friday. Another conundrum!

The Christ later emerged as risen from the dead and ascended to heaven (John 20;1-29; Acts 1:9-11). His little band of followers grew to become a movement, then a worldwide institution called, the Church, the most powerful earth has ever seen.

The Church expects the Christ to return as warrior-King on a white horse to put down His enemies and rule as KING of Kings and LORD of Lords over the earth with His followers. This is an expectation some unbelievers regard as wishful, fictitious thinking. But in the face of the historical evidence, theistic faith cannot allow itself the luxury of such skeptical thinking. The historic evidence of Christ's claims is overwhelming.

But the question remains, from whence this title of Kingship borne by Jesus of Nazareth, was it invented and conferred upon Him by His followers? Or, this is a reality that far transcends ordinary history into the realm of the supernatural? Let's explore a little more these royal titles of KING and LORD attached to the Christ, especially KING.

The Concept of Kingship

Was this royal title of King invented, and attached to Jesus by His followers? Or He is truly a King pointing to a greater reality that we must seek to understand? To answer these questions, we must see if Jesus and His initial group of followers had any roots in the Hebrew Scriptures.

Since the Church began with Jewish followers of Jesus Christ who Himself is rooted in the Hebrew culture, the answer to the kingly title seems to be an obvious carry-over from the Hebrew culture and Bible. But we need to shake this tree a little more to see what else falls out of it to be sure.

The Bible Jesus and His Jewish and Gentile followers used was the Hebrew Bible, what Christian call, the Old Testament (OT). The Hebrew Bible is fundamentally a compilation of documents unveiling Yahweh's dealings with His people in the context of covenant. It records their encounters with other nations and the treatment received. When treated well, that nation prospered. If they were oppressors, the God of the Hebrews champion their liberation. He is the God to be feared by other nations for He presented Himself to be stronger than all.

The God of the Hebrews distinguished Himself as the only true God in a culture where all nations had many gods. Yahweh presented Himself as exclusive. He is equal to no other being and He shares the stage with no other. His preferred name, I AM WHO I AM (YHWH or Yahweh), rendered in English as Jehovah or LORD (Exod.3:1-14). This God is the uncreated, self-existent One, all-knowing, all-powerful, everywhere present, unchanging in his essence or character. The King over the universe and over Israel.

The concept of *God Almighty, the King who reigns,* came down to Christians from the Hebrew culture and Bible, what Christians called, the Old Testament (OT) and Jews refer to as the *Tanakh*. To fully understand the recurring expression in the OT, *the King who reigns*, we must first grasp how the word, king, was used and understood among the ancient peoples including the Hebrews.

The designation, king, was the title given to a male sovereign, who usually exercised power over an independent nation state and retains the right to confer said royal title and power to his descendants.[1] It is important to note that Israelite kings were also called, "Prince" and the "Lord's Anointed" (1Sam.14:4).

One of the supreme titles by which Israel's God was most frequently known is *the God who reigns*. When Isaiah said the Messiah would be called, "Prince of Peace," it is the same as King of Peace (Isa. 9: 6). The Prince of Peace title was first used by Melchizedek, king of Salem who broke bread with Abraham and blessed him; Abraham paid tithes to him (Gen.14:18-20).

The name Melchizedek carries the meaning, "prince of peace," "king of righteousness." This historical character was king and priest of Jerusalem. He is a type of Jesus Christ who carries the same titles (Psalm 76: 2, 110:4; Heb.7).

Who was Yahweh to Israel? He was Israel's King and much more.[2] He was everything: the only One true God, their Creator, the Covenant-maker, Deliverer, the Mighty Warrior, Protector, Preserver, the God who reigns, the King of glory, the Promise-keeper, and much more. All these titles are supported by the Torah and the entire Tanakh (OT). God was Israel's Shalom, a word that means much more than the English word, "peace." To ancient Hebrews and Jews today, sholom includes well-being, health, prosperity, unity, concord, harmony with God and neighbor.[3] The question should be asked the other way around as well, what was Israel to God (Yahweh)?

Israel was (and still is) God's covenant people, "a treasured possession," "a kingdom of priests," "a holy nation" (Exod.19 3-6). This relationship was intended to be consummated in the coming of the Messiah. But Israel broke covenant and rejected the Messiah because of unbelief (John 1:12).

God formed a new and better covenant through Jesus of Nazareth, the Messiah (Heb.8:6-13). This covenant is realized in the Church. In other words, the mission that was Israel's, that is, the redemptive evangelization of the world for salvation through the Messiah has become the mission of the Church (Matt.28:16-20; Acts 2:29-41). National Israel by reason of their unbelief and rejection of the Messiah has been push back in God's program to the time of the Messiah's Second Advent. At that time the whole nation will have a second chance to embrace their Messiah and they will. God has not cast away His covenant people (Rom.9-11).

So, let me emphasize—God has not broken covenant with Israel; it is the other way around. They broke covenant with God (Deut.28). They removed themselves from God's immediate mission and purpose; they should have been the ones bringing the gospel of salvation the nations. Israel will eventually accept Yeshua as their Messiah at His Second Coming.

The Jesus of the New Testament (NT) comes to us within the context of the Hebrew, Greco-Roman culture; His family, tribe (lineage), and nation (Israel) were uniquely Hebrew (Matt.1:1, 18-25; Luke 1:26-38, 2:1-7). It is evident that the gospel writers made every effort to keep Jesus rooted and tied to the Hebrew culture, and we now know all that was God's doing. We embrace both Old and New Testament records as the inspired Word of God.

The significant offices of leadership in the Hebrew culture were prophet, priest, and king. The nation started out with God being their King. Human leaders were called Judges, beginning with Moses, and ending with Samuel (Exod.18:13-27; 1 Sam.12).

During the period of the judges (1380—1050 B.C.) the nation was a loose confederacy of twelve tribes.[4] The only thread that united them was their faith in Yahweh but even to that they were not faithful; they kept backsliding and ending up in bondage to foreign nations as the book of the judges clearly documents. The judges were predominantly military leaders, liberating the nation from foreign oppression and servitude.

When the nation transitioned to become a more stable monarchy, the office of judge was absorbed and distributed to the priestly, the prophetic, and the kingly offices. The priestly office made judgments concerning worship and public health as it relates to infectious diseases among other things. These functions were assigned to the tribe of Levi.

But certain kings who were God's anointed could approach God on behalf of the people. For example, David and Solomon (1 Chron. 22-29; 2 Chron.6-7). The king could not usurp the function of the priesthood without consequences (2 Chron.26:16-23).

The king unites the nation as their deliverer under God, he leads them into war, and he renders Justice; he collects taxes or revenues, and tributes. People could call on the king for justice or to settle a dispute. For example, Solomon had two women claiming to be the mother of the same child (1Kings 3:16-28).

The prophetic office served as the voice of God to the nation, the voice of justice and mercy (Mic.6:8). The prophets tried to keep the nation within the guardrails of the Law of God, speaking truth to the powerful and defending the plight of the poor.

The prophet confronts and rebukes the unjust, even kings when they step out of bounds and act unjustly as we see with Nathan and David, Elijah and Ahab or Jeremiah and Zedekiah (2 Sam.11-12; 1Kings 21; Jer.32). The office of the king, the priest, and the prophet were national institutions in ancient Israel.

King David A Type of Christ?

King David was the greatest king to lead the Hebrew nation. He was not a perfect man; he had failings that would cause the best of us to blush. The text of scripture being honest, did not cover up David's failings, but expose them to the light of history for succeeding generations to see and learn from.

Despite his failings, David, to some extent, is a type of Christ, the Messiah. David was God's anointed King of whom God declares to be a man after His own heart. That statement speaks volumes as to how God felt about this man. David was a rare gem among men but like all of us, he was flawed.

David was the embodiment of the three national offices: prophet, priest, and king. As king, he was a great warrior and deliverer. As priest, he was an exemplary worshipper and representative of God. He contributed more to Israel's worship than any other person. His contributions include: the architectural drawing for the temple, financing of the temple including his personal wealth, song book for worship, organization of choirs, and the selection musical instruments, to name a few. Yet, David had respect for the priesthood, an institution ordained by God.

As prophet, many of his utterances are prophetic statements are fulfilled in Jesus Christ the Messiah. The apostle Peter quoted David on the day of Pentecost, the Lord said unto my Lord, sit thou on my right hand until I make your enemies your footstool (Act 2:25-36;Psalm 16:1-11). Throughout the Psalm, David frequently speaks of God as the King who reigns or coming to reign and that King points to the Messiah, God's anointed One.

For example, Psalm 2 is commonly regarded as messianic. "The kings of the earth rise up and the rulers band together against the LORD and against his Anointed saying, 'Let us break their chains and throw off their shackles'" (vv.3-3). This is viewed as organized treachery against God and his Anointed One.

The psalmist goes on to record God's response, "The One enthroned in heaven laughs; the Lord scoffs at them. He rebukes them in his anger and terrifies them in his wrath, saying, 'I have installed my king on Zion, my holy mountain'" (vv.4-6). Zion is a reference to Jerusalem, but the Psalm is not just referring to the local king who reigns in Jerusalem, but to the Messiah, God's anointed One, the one whom God defends.

Throughout the Psalm, God is the King who reigns over the universe and over His people Israel and the nation is called to faith, obedience, worship, and loyalty. In Psalm 93 (ESV) Jehovah is the King who "reigns" and is "robed in majesty" and strength and demands loyalty. At times the lines between the human king over Israel and the theocratic King blurs; the distinction is hardly discernible. God joins Himself with His people, even calling Himself: the God of Abraham, Isaac, and Jacob.

In Psalm 95 (ESV), Jehovah is the "great King" who is above all gods, the Creator of the universe and all are invited to come before Him and kneel in worship. In Psalm 97 and 99 (ESV) we are simply reminded the, the LORD reigns. In Psalm 145 and 149 the people of God are invited to extol their "God and King" and rejoice in Him.

The prophet Isaiah sums it up for us, he peaks of the Messiah as the Divine King coming to reign from Jerusalem over the earth sitting on the throne of David (Isa.9:6-7). In other words, the God of the Old Testament, the Creator, the King who reigns, Israel's Deliverer, Provider, Protector, the One who is worshiped has come to us in the person of Jesus Christ (John 1:1-3, 14). It is one story that has unfolded in Old Testaments and finds its fulfillment in the New Testament in Jesus Christ, the Anointed One. The King who reigns has come to us in the person of Jesus Christ.

The heavenly messengers to the shepherds on the Judean hills got it right when they sang, "Glory to God in the highest heaven, and on earth peace to those on whom his favor rest" (Luke 2:13-4). What was the message? "Today... a Savior has been born to you; he is the Messiah, the Lord..." (v.11).

The wisemen also got it right when they asked, "Where is the one who has been born King of the Jews? We saw his star when it rose and have come to worship him" (Matt.2:1-2). The wisemen's attitude toward the Christ child and the gifts offered confirmed that this child was indeed Savior, Lord, and King (vv.11-12).

But Herod got it wrong, Jesus did not come to take Herod's throne. So, the murderous massacre he ordered his soldiers to carry out was unnecessary (Matt.2:16-18).

The concept of Jesus Christ being King is not a Christian invention attached to Him to make Him look good, as some would have us believe. The concept of Jesus, the Messiah being King is not only firmly rooted in the Hebrew Bible, it is also the perfect fulfillment of Hebrew Scriptures.

At the crucifixion site of Jesus, the Roman governor posted this inscription on the cross of Jesus over His head: "Jesus of Nazareth, King of the Jews." That was the charge against Him. The Hebrew Bible clearly states that the Messiah would be King. Since He is Jewish, it follows that He would be King of the Jews. The irony is, those that were best qualified to interpret the Hebrew scriptures shouted the loudest to have Him executed; yes, they shouted vociferously to deny Him the title of King (John 19:19-22).

Summary

Israel's Messiah, the Anointed One, was long spoken of by Israel's prophets to be King over His people. The Hebrew Scriptures present Messiah as deliverer, one who carries the title of King. Therefore, Yeshua, Yahweh's anointed One was declared to be King long before the Christian Church was founded.

Jesus of Nazareth was identified by the Hebrew prophet, John the Baptist as the true Messiah (Luke 3:16-21; John 1:19-34). John the Baptist's disciples accepted Jesus as the Messiah (John 1:35-51). And Jesus Himself claimed to be the Messiah of whom the Hebrew prophets speak (Luke 4:14-23).

The question is, why did Jesus of Nazareth, the Messiah, not exert His Kingly authority to liberate His own people from the oppressive Roman yoke? Why did He not restore the glory of Israel back to the golden years of David and Solomon as all Israelites expected Messiah to do?

Why did Jesus, the Messiah, the Anointed of God not resisted dying such shameful death on Roman gallows, if He were indeed the King of the Jews? We have answered one question, but we are now faced with others, even more troubling.

CHAPTER 2

UNDERSTANDING JESUS' KINGSHIP AND KINGDOM

Overview

The Hebrew Bible we Christians call, the Old Testament (OT), presents Yahweh as KING over the universe in general, and King over Israel in particular. It is His Kingdom, and He rules by rights of Creator and Owner (Psalm 24:1). The creation came into being through the blessed Holy Trinity (Gen.1-2; John 1:1-3,14; Col.1:16-

17). And even though God gives governance to humans; they are tenants, not owners (Psalm 8:3-9).

God also exercise Kingly rule over His people Israel. His rule over the created order is His natural Kinship, whereas His rule over His people is His spiritual Kingship. Spiritual kingship is established in the hearts of people, not done by external force.

Again, spiritual Kingship has to do with the rule of God in the hearts of His people through a covenant relationship. On God's part, the covenant is irrevocable, but on Israel's part it is conditioned on faith and obedience expressed in the worship of Yahweh only (Exod.20:1-8; Deut.6:4-8,28:1-68). For the full blessings of the covenant to be realized, three essentials are necessary: faith, obedience, and worship. These are evidence of Yahweh's spiritual rule in the heart of His people.

For this reason, idolatry was the number one sin, because it violates all three core essentials. The commandments begin with acknowledging Yahweh as the one true and living God, Creator and possessor of heaven and earth. God is supreme, sovereign. Israel should not give loyalty or worship to any other or carved any image and claim it to be God (Exod.20:1-7; Deut.6:4-5).

Yahweh first sought to establish His rule in the hearts of His people, for it is not easy to rule over people created as free moral agents if they do not want it. Forced obedience is not obedience; it is rebellion suppressed. Obedience must be out of love, from the heart; it cannot be forced. That is one reason, God's covenant relationship with His people is liken to a marriage (Isa.54: 5-7;

Hose.2:16-20). Love and faithfulness (fidelity) are the cement that holds a marriage or covenant relation together.

Israel defaulted in their part of the covenant relationship in terms of faith, obedience, and worship. For that reason, God promised to forge a new covenant in which his law would be written internally on their hearts (Jer.31:31-34; Heb.8: 6-13). This would make faith, obedience, and worship from the heart more achievable, because the Holy Spirit would make the inner sanctum His dwelling (John 14:15-17, 16:13-15). What the law written on tables of stone could not do, the indwelling Holy Spirit is able to accomplish (Acts 1:8; Rom.8:3-4).

Sin is a heart problem, a condition rooted in human nature; it must be dealt with from within. "The heart is deceitful...and desperately wicked," Jeremiah warns (Jer.17:9 KJV). That is what cause idolatry and backsliding and the loss of the Davidic Kingdom. God would restore the kingdom to Israel under the coming Messiah, but Messiah must first establish His Kingship or rule in the inner sanctum of His people, or they will have the same outcome of loss as before. The Messiah came and His message was the kingdom of heaven is at hand (same as kingdom of God).

Kingdom Rule Misunderstood

The Old Testament laid the groundwork for the spiritual rule of God to be full established with the arrival of Messiah. John the Baptist was the last prophet preparing Israel for the Messiah. He personally introduced the Messiah to Israel.

John's message was "Repent and be baptized for the kingdom of heaven is at hand" (Matt.3:1-6). What does that mean? It means, the spiritual rule of God in the hearts of His people is near you. Jesus arrived, and He preached the same message, "Repent, for the kingdom of heaven is at hand" (Matt.4:17). Jesus is the personification of God's salvation to Israel and the world (John 3:16). The very name Jesus means Savior (Matt.1:21).

The spiritual rule of God in the heart of His people was not a message easily understood by Israel. The religious leaders did not understand the Hebrew Bible in those terms. They were accustomed to God ruling over a natural, geographic, territorial kingdom, such as David and Solomon ruled over. That is the kingdom Israel's leaders expected the Messiah to restore upon His arrival. Yes, Messiah will restore that territorial rule, but after He establishes spiritual rule in the hearts of His people. That was the mission of Jesus at His first coming.

The Messiah Taught by Example

Jesus wanted His people to understand that the kingdom of heaven (same as kingdom of God) is not just God's rule over the universe or over Israel. God has no problem with geographical rule.

His problem is with the heart of unbelieving and rebellious people over which He has not been given rule. The inner sanctum, the domain of the heart is the domain the Messiah came to establish His rule. This is the region of the spiritual kingdom; the domain God wants to rule in, the hearts of His own people and all humankind.

When Jesus said, the kingdom of God is in you, He is referring to God's spiritual rule in the heart. The heart was understood then to be the center of a person's being. Thus, the sayings, "keep thine heart with all diligence for out of it are the issues of life," or "As a man thinks in his heart so is he," (Prov. 4:23, 23:7 KJV).

This inner spiritual rule of God in the heart was an alien concept, not easily understood by the ancient Israelites. But Jesus wanted it understood, received, and implemented because this was necessary for the geographical Kingdom to be restored to Israel. Jesus' mission was first, to save His own people from spiritual bondage to sin and Satan. Salvation was offered to the "Jews first" (Rom.1:16). Jesus was primarily sent to the Jews, and for that reason He first commissioned His disciples to go to "the lost sheep of the house of Israel" (Matt.10: 1-8, 15:24).

But the broader mission was to seek and to "save the lost" of all nations (Matt.18:11, 28:19-20; Acts 1:8). Israel's rejection appears to speed up the mission to the broader mission field.

The first leg of His mission was a spiritual one. But how was He going to get this message understood, received, and embraced? Only the Messiah, the Holy Spirit anointed One could undertake this massive challenge of winning the hearts of people.

First, the Messiah needed to convince His own people that He is indeed the true Messiah of whom the Law, the Prophets, and the Writings bore witness. He must convince them that He is the bodily fulfillment of the Hebrew Scriptures. He started His mission in His hometown synagogue of Nazareth, but He was not well received

(Luke 4:14-30). The record shows that He continued this effort even after His resurrection (Luke 24:25-32).

Second, He gave a new, fresh understanding to the Hebrew Scriptures, beginning with the Sermon on the Mount (Matt.5-7). He made it clear that the essence of the Law of God is love for God and love for neighbor (Matt.5:31-48; John 13: 34-35). But he redefines neighbor to mean more than a person living close to your house, next of kin, family, or tribe but all humankind, even your enemies (Matt.5: 43-48; Luke 10: 28-37).

Third, Jesus redefines righteousness from mere doing the external duties of the law, done to attract the attention and praise of others to oneself to a focus on the inner sanctum. The spiritual vessel out of which we serve God and others must be clean. This is a higher standard of righteousness. Except your righteousness go beyond that of the Scribes and Pharisees, you cannot enter the kingdom of God or heaven (Matt.5:20).

Fourth, to enter this spiritual kingdom of God's rule goes beyond being born physically to the Abraham genealogical line, you must have a spiritual birth from above to be a citizen in this new thing God is doing (John 3:1-16).

Fifth, the spiritual kingdom of God's rule is mysterious. It cannot be observed by the physical eyes, that you can say it is here or there (Luke 17:20-21). It is as selective as a fisherman's net thrown into the sea; it catches all kinds of fish, some are selected, some are thrown back (Matt.13: 47-50). The kingdom of heaven is unique as a farmer sowing seeds; some fall by the wayside and are devoured by birds, some fall among thorns, some spring up but due to shallow soil wither away. But others fall on good ground and produce a harvest (Matt.13:3-8,18-23, 24-30).

Sixth, the spiritual kingdom of God is precious and hidden, but discoverable. Jesus expresses it this way, the kingdom of heaven is like a treasure hidden in a field, after a man finds it, he buries it again, and with joy sold all he has and buy that field (vv.44). This parable teaches four things about the kingdom: 1) It is precious, worth possessing, 2) it is hidden, yet discoverable, 3) It is demanding but worth owning, 4) It must be personally discovered to possessed.

As a rule of life, precious things hardly come revealed or exposed for easy pickings. Diamonds, gold, silver, copper, or even oil, all require serious digging to uncover. These precious commodities are rewards for those who are willing to do the inquiry of serious spadework. The same is true of the kingdom of God; it is a hidden treasure that demands serious investment if you want to own it. It demands something of you, your life's investment. It is like a treasure hidden in a field.

To own the field, you must sell all that you have and buy it. He who owns the field owns the treasure. The field becomes your single investment. Your loyalty is no longer divided because wherever a person's treasure is, there is his heart also, Jesus asserted (Matt.6:19-21).

Note that the treasure must be personally discovered and personally owned; the same is true of eternal life (John 3:16). You must be willing to sell all that you have to own this treasure. The rich young ruler discovered eternal life; it is resident in the person of Jesus Christ. But the young man was not willing to unload his own baggage to make this investment, so he walked away lost and despondent. Jesus made the same demand on national Israel, and they rejected Him. It is the same demand made on all of us that seek eternal life. It is the sixth mystery of the spiritual kingdom.

Seventh, the spiritual kingdom of God's rule calls for a different kind of worship that is all inclusive of those beyond the borders of Israel. It is not limited to worship in one local geography as the Jewish temple (John 4:19-24; Acts 1:8).

Eighth, the kingdom of God is not Just for the elite and privilege, in fact they stand the risk of being cast out. It is for the poor, the widow, the fatherless, the stranger, all those who have been excluded from your present worship system (Matt.8:11-12).

Ninth, the spiritual kingdom is sustained by the bread of life, and the water of life. Jesus is that water and bread that all in Israel must partake to be saved (John 6: 44-58).

Messiah Kinship Rejected

Despite His ministry efforts, Jesus was rejected by His own people. He did not meet the Messiah expectation of Israel's elite, religious class (John 1:12). Yet, the common people gladly received His message, but their expectation was no different from the elite class. Just what was their expectation?

First, they did not believe their own Scripture concerning the Messiah. Yeshua fulfills all the Scriptures of the Hebrew Bible concerning the Messiah. Even the heathen, debauched king Herod exercised more faith in the Hebrew Scriptures than Israel's religious leader. When the Magi arrived at his palace in the dead of night, making inquiry for the Christ child who was born King of the Jews, Herod sent for the religious leaders. They came to his palace with their scrolls, identified the Christ Child ancestral lineage, the city of and location of his birth and went back to bed.

The Magi used that information to locate the Christ Child and Herod used the same information to carry out a massacre of children in Bethlehem, when he found out that the Magi outwitted him and did not return to him. How come the religious leaders were not in the least curious to send a delegation to check out the story. The Hebrew Scriptures connected all the dots pointing to Jesus of Nazareth as the Messiah, but they did not care.

Second, from birth Jesus was distinguished as the Messiah. There is the Mary and Joseph story. They knew the virgin's story but did not believe it because they accused Jesus of being born of fornication. They called Him illegitimate to His face (John 8: 41). Because they did not believe what the prophets of their own Scriptures prophesied. The shepherd' story was no secret, they broadcast it far and wide, but it did not matter to the religious elite (Luke 2: 8-18). We have no record of an investigation been done by the Sanhedrin because they didn't care.

Third, the story of the Child's dedication in the temple and the prophecy spoken of Him should have stirred some curiosity among religious leaders who were waiting for the Messiah (Luke 2:22-40). How could they miss this unparallel opportunity? No wonder this same child grew up to call them blind guides, blind leading the blind (Matt.23:13-29).

Fourth, at age twelve Mary and Joseph took the boy Jesus to Jerusalem to celebrate His Bar Mitzvah and the Passover; this was a dramatic event from Nazareth to Jerusalem and back. And the drama was no secret to the religious authorities because the boy Jesus was missing for three days while Mary and Joseph searched desperately through the city for Him.

And at last, they found Him in the temple! He was among the experts of the Law asking and answering question that stunned these learned men. Yet, they did not discern that they were talking to the Messiah (Luke 2:41-52). Had they, the Israel's history would have been different.

Fifth, the ministry work of Jesus His baptism to His death and resurrection and ascension is fraught with untold miracles that this is the Messiah, the King of Israel. His ministry work bear witness as to who but they refused to believe.

They knew the truth, and sought to eradicate it, but it kept surfacing and the covered it up. The evidence is too overwhelming for intelligent people to claim ignorance.

Sixth, perhaps they would have acknowledged Him as their Messiah, had He chosen to be crowned King on their own terms which would have compromised His messianic the mission and put Him outside the will of God. Israel refused Jesus establishing the rule of God in their heart and that postponed the Davidic kingdom that they so desperately wanted restored.

Seventh, God through the Messiah raised up a new entity called, the Church. Through the Church God through Jesus Christ is establishing His spiritual rule in the heart of every human group on earth. And when the time is right, the Messiah will return as KING of Kings and LORD of Lords to sit upon the throne of David and rule over the earth. All Israel that receive Him as their Messiah and Savior will be saved; there is no salvation without Jesus Christ.

Eight, in fulfillment of Jesus' Matthew 24 prophecy, the Roman army in 70 A.D. gave the death blow to *First Century* Judaism. Jerusalem was ransacked, the temple destroyed, sacrifices ceased, Ark of the Covenant and scrolls vanished, priesthood in shambles, and thousands upon thousands of Jews killed and taken prison from Jerusalem.

Overtime Judaism reinvented itself without the use of the temple and sacrifice, among other things, but it never changed the old lie about Jesus of Nazareth until this day. The spiritual blindness toward the Messiah will continue for national Israel until His second advent the Christ.

There are individual Jews, however, who have acknowledged Jesus as the true Messiah and have come to find salvation from sin in Him. We call them messianic Jews; they are part of the Church, though maintaining their Jewish heritage.

Summary

God has no difficulty establishing His rule over the Universe, geographically. Establishing spiritual rule in the hearts of humankind is the challenging venture. Why is that, isn't God all-powerful? Yes, He is Almighty and much more.

But God created humans as free moral agents. He created them in His image and likeness which includes rational intelligence, the power of reason and choice. He created human for Himself, as part of His family and for His glory and praise. He chose to respect the gift of free will He endowed on them.

To establish His spiritual rule in human hearts, it cannot be forced from without; it must come from within. In other words, it must flow out of a voluntary choice of love, faith, obedience, and worship. Perhaps, not all humans will want to respond to the Creator that way. But as risky as that may be, it is the only way to deal with a being with the power of choice.

God through love and patience has given humans enough time weigh his options, think it through, and make his choice as to who or what spiritual authority will rule his heart for time and eternity.

Choices come with rewards and consequences; this has been made clear from the paradise garden. Our ancestral parents were given a choice with rewards and consequences. The result of their choice was not hidden from them. They were shown the tree of life and the tree of death. They were told not to eat from the tree of death for the outcome would be death. But with eyes wide opened, they exercised their freedom of choice as to who or what would exercise spirituality rule over them. For that reason, God put the backup plan of redemption in place. If human made a choice that brings sorrow, he will, at least get a second chance to eat of the tree of life by exercising his will another way.

What we learned through the debacle of our ancestral parents' choice is that there are two spirit beings who exercise spiritual paternity over human life and all of us have the freedom to choose which will rule over us. God will help us to make the right choice, but He will not force or overrule us. Jesus said to one group of people, "you are of your father the devil" (John 8:44). This is spiritual paternity by choice. With eyes wide-open, Israel made the wrong choice. That has consequences, but they will be given a second chance upon the return of the Christ (Rom.9-11; Rev.7).

Jesus teaches that there is a broad road and a narrow road, one leads to destruction and the other leads to life, eternal life. That eternal life is resident in Jesus Christ the Son of God (John 3:16; 10:10b). Jesus is the way to eternal life, and it starts when He establish the rule of God in our hearts with the assistance of the blessed Holy Spirit. That is what is meant by the kingdom of God is in you. Only those humans whom God has established His rule in their hearts will reign with Him in the earthly, geographical kingdom when Messiah returns.

The kingdom of God (the rule of God) has come in us, and it is coming among us, geographically. Those of us who have the spiritual rule of God in our hearts are instructed by the King to pray, "thy Kingdom come, thy will be done on earth as it is in heaven" (Matt.6:9-10). This speaks of the geographical rule of God over the earth through Jesus Christ when all enemies are forever put down when and where no contenders are allowed.

This is how the dual aspects of the kingdom of God is to be understood: the spiritual kingdom of God establishing His rule in our hearts, and the natural, geographical kingdom where God's rule and will flourish without the opposition of any contending king and kingdom. As Handel so aptly noted in his classic repertory, the

Messiah, When Jesus comes, the kingdoms of this world will become the kingdom of our God and of His Christ.

CHAPTER 3

KINGSHIP IMPOSED AND DECLINED

A Conflict of Visions

Why did the Jews reject Jesus Christ as their Messiah? This question is answered in the previous chapter. But let us summarize that rejection from a slightly different perspective. Fundamentally, they rejected Jesus because they had a different vision of the Messiah's person and mission than the Messiah had of Himself; that constituted a serious visions conflict.

What was the Hebrew's vision of the Messiah? In as much as the Hebrew Scriptures present the Messiah in human and divine terms, they did not expect the Messiah to be divine. Therefore, when the Christ came and claimed to have had an existence prior to Abraham and referring to Himself as the Son of God, they accused Him of speaking blasphemously.

The idea of the Messiah giving His life for the redemption of both Jews and gentiles was unthinkable to the Jews, yet ironically, not alien to the text of the Hebrew Bible, God's written revelation to them (Isa.9:6-7; 53:1-12).

So, what did they expect their Messiah to be? They expected a deliverer, a heroic and liberating personality like Moses, Gideon, and David, an anointed man on whom God's favor rests. He would lead the charge in battle to free them from all oppressors, including the Romans. Messiah would not only free them from the Roman yoke, he would also restore the golden years of Israel in keeping with their understanding of the Abrahamic, Mosaic, and Davidic covenants.

Additionally, the Jews had the narrow vision of the Messiah just restoring the natural kingdom to Israel with well-defined borders such as were laid out by Moses and Joshua (Jos. 1:1-6). They had no vision of a worldwide spiritual kingdom in which God establish His rule in the hearts of humankind. They failed to understand that Israel lost the natural, geographical kingdom because the rule of God did not take root in their hearts.

What was Jesus' vision of Himself, His mission, and His people? Jesus sees Himself as the Son of Man, the Son of God, the One of whom the Hebrew Scriptures speaks. He sees Himself as the incarnate Son of God, the One appointed to carry out Yahweh's vision for His people and the world. His mission was to first establish a spiritual kingdom. That is the rule of God in the hearts of humankind, the Jew first then the gentiles. Jesus would accomplish this by giving His life for the redemption of Israel and of all humankind (John 3:16). Berkhof refers to this as "the spiritual kingship of Christ" through which Christ exercises royal rule over the *regnum gratiae*, that is over His people."[1]

After the establishment of the spiritual kingdom, God would establish His natural Kingdom on the earth, what Israel refers to as the restoration of the Davidic kingdom. God's vision is to restore the Davidic Kingdom through His Son, but the restoration would not be limited to the borders of Israel and exclusively for ethnic Jews. Yes, they would play a significant role in all this. But Christ's Kingship will not be just over Israel; it will be worldwide, but His throne will be in Jerusalem (Isa.9:6-7).

The kingdom of God is not just territorial or geographical; it has a spiritual dimension. You could say it is an interior kingdom in which Christ establishes the rule of God in the hearts of humans. "The kingdom of God is in you," Jesus said (Luke 17:21). Without the establishment of this interior kingdom, it is not possible to rule humans without brute force.

But brute force is not God's governance vision for His world that he created in love and redeemed in love; He must also govern or rule in of love. Love rules from the heart. People serve because they want to serve, not because they are forced to serve. A kingdom ruled by brute force has a deficit in love and freedom.

For these reasons, on the night of the Last Supper, Jesus poured water into a basin and began to wash His disciples' feet, demonstrating that greatness in the kingdom of God is serving God and neighbor in love and humility. While doing that He said, "A new command I give unto you: Love one another. As I have loved you, so you must one another." He goes on to say, "By this everyone will know that you are my disciples, if you love one another " (John 13: 1-17, 34-35).

In the spiritual kingdom, God writes His laws in the hearts of humankind, not on tables of stone. Israel loss the natural kingdom because they were not won inwardly to the Lord. God through the Messiah was doing a new thing, not resuscitating and old , failed approach. It is a new covenant based upon new laws, better promises, a different priesthood, better sacrifice (Heb.7-10).

Even though the Jewish religious elite and Jesus had opposing visions concerning the restoration of the Davidic Kingdom: one theological and the other political, the religious elite thought they could negotiate the theological question, but the political question was unnegotiable.

The elites were members of the Sanhedrin, the final authority on Jewish life; they thought Jesus would eventually come around to their views. But they were wrong, grossly mistaken. Jesus was not and could not capitulate to their view. That is exactly what Satan wanted Him to do, abandon His redemptive mission put in place by the Father from eternity and now executed in time.

Furthermore, the religious elite that requires that compromise was a backslidden, spiritually blind bunch who already substituted the Word of God for the traditions of men. Jesus could not suspend God's vision for His people and the world to satisfy this backslidden, religious elite. There would be no compromise on the theological or the political question.

God's mission through Jesus Christ would be discharged exactly as foretold in the Hebrew Scriptures. This finally came to a head during Passover week A.D.30, the week of His passion.

Kingdoms in Conflict

Palm Sunday, the beginning of Passover week A.D. 30, Jesus headed a procession from the peasant village of Nazareth in Galilee, down the Mount of Olives into Jerusalem. He rides on a donkey in fulfillment of Zacharias prophecy, he represents the kingdom of God, His followers are peasants, jubilant cheering and waving palm branches and shouting, "Hosana to the Son of David! Blessed is he who comes in the name of the Lord!" (Matt.21:9).

According to Mark Oakley, Canon of Saint Paul's Cathedral in a sermon--on the other side of town, the same day, an imperial procession entered Jerusalem, led by Pontius Pilate, the Roman Governor, coming from the governor's mansion in Caesarea. He leads calvary of Roman soldier on war horses, sword and spears and shields. He comes to reinforce the Roman garrison that overlooks the Jewish temple in Jerusalem. This reinforcement is there just "in case there is any trouble" as the Jews celebrate their liberation from another empire. Two processions representing two different kingdoms: the kingdom of God and Caesar's kingdom. One a kingdom of peace and good will for all, the other a kingdom of power, violence, force, and war. These two kingdoms will collide this Passover week, Oakley noted.[2]

Caiaphas and his cronies merged their interests with Caesar's kingdom, not the kingdom of God. They wanted Jesus dead! So, he had Jesus arrested on false charges and when the Roman Governor found Him innocent of all charges, Caiaphas stirred up the people to demand the release of a known criminal named, Barabbas. He demanded execution for Jesus, despite His innocence. Caiaphas, Israel's high priest led the chant to crucify Jesus. He loudly proclaimed, "We have no king but Caesar!" He was wittingly or unwittingly doing Satan's biddings (John 19:6-12).

Satan had already breached the inner circle of Jesus' little group; he entered Judas's heart while he shared a meal with the Jesus and the other disciples. Judas excused himself and went to cut the betrayal deal with Caiaphas (Matt.26:14-16). Hours later, Jesus was arrested, Peter His ardent spokesman, denied knowing Him and the others, except John, ran like scared rabbits.

Jesus, the Sum of Israel's Leadership

Israel had four national, leadership titles: judge, prophet, priest, and king. As pointed out earlier, in the process of time the role of the judge ceased as singular office and its role absorbed by the other three offices. Jesus the Messiah personifies all four official functions: Judge, Prophet, Priest, and King.

But Christians tend to push back the full exercise of Christ's judgeship and kingship titles to time of His second advent. At least that is the way most Christian Bible scholars and theologians perceived it throughout the history of the Church. But how did Jesus perceive Himself regarding the use of these titles?

It is evident that the self-understanding of the Messiah, God's anointed One, was in line with the Hebrew prophets, but not in line with the expectations of the religious elite of Israel. When Jesus first appeared on the scene at the Jordan, He wanted John to baptize Him to fulfill all righteousness. In other words, Jesus saw Himself as the fulfillment of the Hebrew Scriptures.

A little later in Nazareth He read from the scroll of the Prophet Isaiah and made it clear that He fulfills the prophetic utterances read that day in the hearing of that congregation. That claim horrified the worshippers who knew Him and His family. They considered His claim preposterous and blasphemous and took actions to expel him out of the synagogue (Luke 4:14-30).

His hometown folks rejected His claim to messiahship, that included His own brothers. By the time of His Palm Sunday procession into Jerusalem, the Jewish religious elite, the Sanhedrin in particular, were convinced that Jesus was an imposter and were bent on destroying Him. The Sanhedrin was the official body that interpreted the Scriptures and guided the nation under God. But to Jesus, they had gone rogue.

If they rejected Jesus as Messiah, the whole nation would follow suit. The religious elite carefully studied Jesus from a theological and political perspective. They would have claimed Him as their Messiah, but Jesus' political interest did not match those of the religious elite; they could not take the risk to cooperate with a political revolutionary of whom they were not certain. All previous uprising were crushed by the Roman legion, and they retained their privileged status only because it was clear they were not part of such uprising.

But Jesus was different. He appears to have powers no one else had. Such powers could be useful to deliver what they wanted, but Jesus did not share their interest. He was not willing to play their game and could not because their interests run counter to His mission. Unable to secure ironclad guarantee in terms of the Messiah's interest and attitude, they turned against Him. To them, Jesus became more of a threat than Israel's hope.

But as the common people listened and observed Jesus, they began to come to the realization that He must be the true Messiah. For that reason, they gladly received His message. But below the surface, their expectations were unwittingly no different from the religious elite. Like the religious elite, they too wanted deliverance from the Roman yoke and the restoration of the golden years of the Davidic kingdom. And they were pragmatic about it, because they did not care how Jesus secure such victory; the method was of small concern to them.

Ironically, Jesus was indeed the true Messiah to accomplish all that heavy lifting God's way and in God's time. And that was no great mystery, for the process is prophetically laid out in Hebrew Scriptures (Isa.9:6-7). Had they not cast aside the Word of God for the traditions of men, they would have recognized Jesus as their Messiah. The religious elite were no fools; they were learned men, but with eyes wide opened, they rejected Jesus and that made them fools. He did not meet their expectations (John 1:12).

Enticement of Jesus Being King by Popular Expectations.

But just what was the religious elite's expectations? At the risk of being redundant, lets state it again. The plan to throw off the Roman yoke must be ironclad and foolproof; it must have the guarantee of succeeding, not failed as other half-baked, Barabbas type revolutions. In this sense, their thinking was sober minded, because the Roman Legion was no pushover and a failed attempt involving the religious elite would doom their privileged lifestyle and the future of all Israel. The stakes were very high.

Their expectations are best summed up as human effort to make Jesus King on their own terms. When analyzed and fully understood, their expectations equal that of Satan's, cleverly camouflaged. But it is God who will restore the kingdom to Israel in His time, not the Sanhedrin or any handpicked, religious, or political revolutionary approved by them (Acts 1:6-7).

Satan wanted to give the religious elite their expectation, even without they knowing it is Satan's doing. This clever Satanic plot is woven through at least five major opportunities presented to Jesus to be the geographical Messiah-King over Israel and perhaps the world. Satan first made the offer to Jesus at the end of His forty-day fast (Matt.4:8-10). It was an attractive offer any ambitious leader would find difficult to refuse, but Jesus was not any ambitious leader. Jesus had no parallel; He is God incarnate (John 1:1-3, 14). The earth is already His (Psalm24:1; Col.1:15-20).

We will now look at these five major attempts to seduce Jesus Christ to become king on terms different from His mission assignment and different from that which the Hebrew Scriptures prophetically laid out. In these scenarios, Jesus, the Messiah, would forego God establishing spiritual rule in the hearts of humans. This is an attempt to abort redemption all together.

First, Satan offers to make Jesus King. Satan is one of the most ambitious of created beings, but he was not created as Satan but as a beautiful, exalted, glorious, and high-ranking angel. His selfish aspiration was to exalt himself above what he was created to be—that led to his downfall and expulsion from heaven (Isa.14:12-15; Ezek.28:12-15; Rev.12:7-11).

Satan is determined to frustrate the purpose of God in creation and redemption. This is evident in his attempt to corrupt angels and humans (Gen.3; Rev.12). He will continue this way until he is disposed of in the lake of burning sulfur (Rev.20:10).

After deceiving our ancestral parents in the *Paradise Garden,* Satan sought to corrupt the godly line through which the Messiah should come. When that did not work, Satan sought to destroy Israel, the nation through which the Messiah would come, using nations like Egypt, Assyria, Babylon, Persia, Rome, and then Nazi Germany. There are several Arab and none-Arab nations that still have their bow bent against Israel and will make their move when the time is right for them.

When Israel's Messiah arrived, Satan had several parallel schemes at work to kill, deceive, bribe, and derail God's purpose. These schemes were directed at the Messiah Himself, His followers, and against Israel (Rev.12). We will not give space in this work to elaborate on all these schemes; we will just explore two parallel tracks: one to kill, the other to deceive. Jesus said, Satan comes to steal, kill, and destroy (John 10:10a).

Satan sought to kill the Christ child from cradle to Calvary. He thought he succeeded at the cross until the resurrection proved him wrong. But if you return to the birth of Christ, you see Satan at work trying to kill the Christ child. King Herod had the children of Bethlehem massacred in his effort to kill Jesus, whom he thought was a rival king for his throne (Matt.2). Mary, Joseph, and the child Jesus became refugees in Egypt, trying to escape the wrath of king Herod (vv.13-18). Throughout His early ministry, Satan used a multi-track approach in his effort to kill Jesus. He infiltrated the ministry team of Jesus, destroyed Judas, and brought down Peter.

On the deception track, Satan thought deceiving Jesus would accomplish his diabolical purpose just as effectively as killing Him. This is seen in the temptation of Jesus, shortly after His baptism. Satan offered to make Jesus King over the kingdoms of this world if Jesus would worship him. Jesus declined his offer of deception and bribery (Matt.4:8-11). Being king is about power and glory. Jesus was presented with this attraction in different ways. But Satan was the first to make the offer.

Second, Jesus was given the opportunity to become King on the terms of the religious elite of His people. The religious elite would have made Jesus King, had He chosen to do it on their terms. The High Priest and most members of the Sanhedrin would have used Jesus if He were willing to play the proverbial ball.

These men were no fools; they enjoyed a comfortable living by accommodation with the Roman government, and they were not willing to risk that. Nor were they willing to risk losing their temple and way of life for some half-baked, ill-advised, Barabbas type revolutionary movement. They had seen many would be revolutionaries crushed by the Roman authorities before. Jesus was different; He had powers no one had. But they were not convinced that Jesus could pull off a successful revolution if it were not done their way. They must be the benefactors and beneficiaries of such a restorative move of bring back the golden years of David and Solomon to Israel.

These lettered men of scholarship studied Jesus every move but could not comprehend Him and could not outwit Him. They vetted Jesus to see if He was right for such a role. But Jesus did not pass their test and was posing a risk to them.

Jesus kept talking about some abstract Kingdom, not the restoration of the Kingdom of David and Solomon. He talks about, my kingdom is not of this world. These men only know of this world. Jesus pays taxes and was friendly to tax collectors. He upset the lucrative temple business. He was too sympathetic to Caesar's government; we can't trust Him. Jesus was not willing to play their game and they turned against Him for he was too great a threat to them.

Third, the common people wanted to take Jesus by force and make Him King (John 6:14-15). The common people received Jesus gladly. They believed He was the Messiah and were ready to seize and make Him king, but for the wrong reasons. One such occasions was after the feeding of the five thousand. Jesus ministered to their physical and spiritual needs: He preach the good news of the kingdom of God, he healed those who were sick, delivered those possessed by demons, and provided them a feast of bread and fish (John 1-13).

After the people saw this miraculous sign of bread and fish among other things they said, "Surely this is the Prophet who is to come into the world." Jesus, knowing that they intended to come and make him king by force, withdrew again to a mountain by himself" (vv.14-15). Jesus pulled Himself away from this crowd because they were ready to crown Him king for the wrong reason.

But they tracked Him down to the far side of the lake and found Him the next day. Upon finding Him, they said, Rabbi we have been search for you! Jesus responded with the hard truth, you are looking for me, not because you were moved by the miraculous signs you saw but because you had your full of bread and fish. Don't labor for the food that spoils, but for the food that endures to eternal life (vv.25-27).

This commenced a long discourse on the bread of life which resulted in many abandoning Jesus (John 6:28-66). They followed Him for the wrong reasons and would have made Him king for the wrong reasons; they had no interest in the kingdom of God that Jesus truly represented. Their vision of spiritual things was no less myopic than that of religious elite that rejected Jesus.

Another group of common folks that would have made Him king is the group that march with Him from Galilee down the Mount of Olive into the city of Jerusalem waving palm branches. This happened on a Spring Day in 30 A.D. when Jesus entered the

Jerusalem on a donkey with a jubilant crowd shouting hosana, hosana! Blessed is he who comes in the name of the Lord. Hosana to the Son of David (Matt.21:1-11).

The religious elite were not convinced by any of this; they had already concluded that Jesus was not their man. And Jesus further outraged them by disrupting the lucrative temple business (vv.12-16). Jesus refused to be king on their terms, and they had to get rid of Him.

Fourth, Jesus was pressured by His own ministry team to restore the kingdom to Israel (Acts 1:6-8). To do this Jesus would have to go against Rome; it is declaring Himself King. This was pressure to act contrary to His mission from within His own ministry group. They kept asking for the restoration of the kingdom to Israel.

Despite His teachings about the kingdom of heaven or the kingdom of God, they could not see beyond the geographical kingdom of Israel once enjoyed under David and Solomon. They wanted the restoration of that kingdom. So, they kept asking Jesus, will you restore the kingdom now to Israel, if not now when? This would involve a revolution more powerful than the Roman army can put down. Jesus refused to be that type of revolutionary. Perhaps, Judas betrayal was an attempt to force His hand but that ended badly.

But by that time the religious elite had already concluded that Jesus was not their man. He was anathema to their hypocritical, elitism, and more a sympathizer of Rome. They feared He was more positioned to bring down the full wrath of Caesar's government on them and destroy their comfortable place of privilege. For that among other reasons, they made the preemptive strike to get rid of Him. And to their delight, their murderous, diabolical plot succeeded with the help of Judas. The betrayal, an inside job.

Despite all that, Jesus did not deny that He is a King, but not over Caesar's kingdom, "My kingdom is not of this world," he said (John 18: 36-37). Pilate, the Roman Governor was satisfied that this man was no personal threat to his position or of any threat to Caesar's government. Jesus had proved His innocence, and Pilate was willing to let him go free (John 19:1-13).

But the Jewish religious elite would have none of this; they threw Pilate a curved ball. The Jewish High Priest shouted over the mob, "We have no king but Caesar, if you let this man go, you are not Caesar's friend" (19:15-16). Hearing that, Pilate capitulated to their demands, uttering these absurd words, "I find no fault in him, but you take him and crucify him" (John 19:6).

Jesus of Nazareth King of the Jews

The Roman governor, Pilate, felt put upon by Caiaphas and His cronies. He knew Jesus was innocent, but they threw him a curved ball threatening his governorship. If he is not will play ball with them, then they will appeal to Caesar. Such appeal, of course, would threaten the governor's position. Most politicians are no different today, political expediency trumps ethics and morality.

In John (19:16-22), his benign protest can be seen on heard in the post he placed over the condemned Messiah's head. "Jesus of Nazareth King of the Jews." But the High Priest said, don't write that, instead write, "He says he is king of the Jews." Pilate in protest said, "What I have written, I have written," translation, it will remain exactly as written (John 19:19-22).

Despite Israel's rejection of Jesus as Messiah/King, He remains King on His terms. Upon His second advent, Israel will finally recognize Jesus as their Messiah/King, but He will also be King of all humankind. It is through Jesus, the seed of Abraham, "all peoples on the earth will be blessed" (Gen.12:3).

The gospel of the kingdom will be preached to all nations through the agency of the Church and all who respond in repentance and faith will not only born again into the kingdom of God and Christ, but His rule will also be established in their hearts. This is the way the blessings of Abraham come upon the gentiles.

Summary

Jesus refused Satan's bribery to make Him king over the kingdoms of this world by worshipping him Satan and thereby avoiding the cross and the redemption of humans.

Jesus refused the religious elite's desire to make Him king on their terms; by so doing He had to face the wrath of Caiaphas and his group. Caiaphas was the most powerful man in all of Israel.

Jesus further rejected the common people's sincere desire to take Him by force and make Him King.

Finally, Jesus He rejected the pressure from His own ministry group to restore the Davidic kingdom to Israel now; that was their way of making Him king whether they realized it or not. All four attempts to make Jesus King were satanic. They were outside the redemptive mission of Christ, and the purpose of God. Jesus had to reject them. National Israel rejected Jesus of Nazareth as their Messiah, and that rejection continues in to the 21st Century.

But despite the rejection of His own people, God through Jesus Christ was at work laying the solid foundation for the spiritual kingdom He came to establish in the hearts of humankind, a kingdom that was the theme of Jesus' ministry.

This kingdom could only be established redemptively through Christ's sacrificial death on the cross, His glorious ascension, and the coming of the blessed Holy Spirit to empower a people to carry the good news of the gospel to the ends of the earth. God was not taken by surprise by Israel's rejection. Because of their rejection, Jesus established the Church, the new people of God.

Despite Israel's wholesale rejection of the Messiah, God has not abandoned them. Israel's blindness is temporary until God's program with the gentiles has run its course (Rom.9-11).

Part II
The Exaltation of the Christ

The coronation of the Christ must be viewed and understood within the context of his exaltation.

CORONATION OF THE CHRIST & THE MARRIAGE SUPPER

The exaltation of the Christ includes His resurrection, His ascension, His session at the right hand of the father, His coronation, and second coming to reign.

CHAPTER 4

EXALTATION OF THE CHRIST EXPLAINED

Overview

The focus of this book is *the coronation of the Christ* and *the marriage supper of the Lamb*. These are not isolated events; they are executed within the broader context of the exaltation and continued glorification of the *Christ*. In other words, the coronation must be understood within the context of Christ's exaltation. The exaltation of the Christ is not a subject frequently preached or taught in local churches; much is not known about it among average believers of the Church.

So, what is the exaltation of the Christ? Noah Webster designates exaltation, a noun, meaning, "the act of raising high." In the primary sense, it is "elevation to power, office, rank, dignity or excellence." In the secondary sense, it means elevated state, state of greatness or dignity.[1] The word is applicable to the Christ in both its primary and secondary sense and more.

Exaltation refers to the Christ being restored to His prior position of power and glory enjoyed with the Father and the blessed Holy Spirit before He became incarnate as Jesus Christ. But it also includes the assumption of positions and functions He did not have before He became incarnate.

Therefore, to understand the coronation, we must first address the exaltation of the Christ and its major themes. They are the resurrection of the Christ, the ascension of the Christ, the reign at the Father's right hand, and the second advent of the Christ in power and glory to reign.

There are several sub-themes as well to understand, such as the priesthood of the Christ, and His judgeship, to name a few. We might make passing reference to other sub-themes but will not entertain detail discussions on them.[2]

We must also say a word or two about the *Second Person* of the Holy Trinity before He became human and took the names, Jesus and Christ. Jesus means Savior or deliverer; Christ means, the anointed One or Messiah (Matt.1:21; Luke 4:1,14-19).

The Preincarnation of the Christ

The Bible and Christian theology teach the preexistence of the Being who took on flesh and became known to us as Jesus Christ. What was His name before He took on flesh and became a man?

We do not know, because the Bible doe does not directly say. But it has much to say about His preexistence as a member of the blessed Holy Trinity. In addressing the preexistence question, the apostle John writes, "In the beginning was the Word [Greek: Logos], and the Word was with God, and the Word was God. He was with God in the beginning" (John 1:1-2). John goes on to say, "The Word became flesh and made his dwelling among us. We have seen his glory, the glory of the one and only Son, who came from the father, full of grace and truth" (v.14).

We also accept that the miraculous conception and birth of the Christ are part of the incarnation process (Matt.1:18-24; Luke 1:26-38). *The Word of God* is the name best associated with His preincarnate state and He returns under that name, *the Word of God*, written on His robe (Rev.2:12,19:13).

The Bible further teaches that the natural world was created by the same Being who took on flesh and became man. For a Being to create the natural world, He must have preexisted, for a house cannot exist before the person that builds it. The apostle John writes, "Through him all things were made; without him nothing was made that has been made" (John 1:3; 1 John 1:1-2).

The apostle Paul speaking of the Christ said, "The Son is the image of the invisible God, the firstborn over all creation. For in him all things were created: things in heaven and on earth.... He is before all things, and in him all things hold together, and he is the head of the body, the church..." (Col.1:15-18).

Furthermore, John the Baptist referenced the preexistence of the Christ in this declaration, "This was He of whom I said, He who comes after me is preferred before me, for He was before me" (John 1:15). John the Baptist's birth age is older than Jesus Christ, so this must be a reference to Christ's preexistence. Jesus Himself said, "Before Abraham was, I am." This claim threw His Jewish audience into uproar, and they responded, "You are not even fifty years old..." and claim to live before Abraham (John 8:57-59).

The process by which the *Second Person* of the blessed *Holy Trinity* became man in the person of Jesus Christ is referred to in Christian theology as the incarnation (in human flesh) or the humiliation of Christ (stepping down). The apostle Paul speaks of the humiliation in the following words:

> In your relationship with one another, have the same mindset as Christ Jesus: Who, being in very nature God, did not consider equality with God something to be used for his own advantage; rather, he made himself nothing by taking the very nature of a servant, being made in human likeness. And being found in appearance as a man, he humbled himself by becoming obedient to death—even death on a cross. (Philip.2:5-8)

In the humiliation process, the *Second Person* of the Trinity laid aside His glory and divested Himself of His Majesty and suspended the exercise of certain non-communicable attributes (e.g., omnipotence, omniscience, and omnipresence - these are attributes not shared with any created being).

He retained all His moral attributes such as holiness, truth, justice, mercy, love, goodness, kindness, to name a few. These are shared with created beings especially humans. The humiliation also includes the Messiah's lowly birth, His suffering, death, and burial. Some scholars include the descent of His soul into *Hades*.

What Is Meant by Exaltation of the Christ?

The exaltation of the Christ is the Second Person of the blessed Holy Trinity taking back all of that which He divested Himself of to become one of us: His glory, His Majesty, and the full exercise of His attributes (omnipotence, omnipresence, omniscience, and much more. The exaltation could also be called, the glorification of the Christ, because He had it all restored, and much more.

I say, "and much more" because the Father has conferred on the man Jesus Christ, positions, titles, and honors He did not have before He became Man. For example, a new name with human personhood, mediator, judge, advocate, and high priest, to name a few. The apostle Paul expresses it this way:

> Therefore, God exalted him to the highest place and gave him the name that is above every name, that at the name of Jesus every knee should bow, in

heaven and on earth and under the earth, and every tongue acknowledge that Jesus Christ is Lord, to the glory of God the Father. (Philip.2:9-11)

Having explained the incarnation, looking at what the Second Person of the blessed Holy Trinity surrendered to become one of us, we can have a better appreciation of His exaltation and what it includes. We will now look at the four major themes of the exaltation of the Christ.

The Resurrection of the Christ

The exaltation of the Christ begins with His bodily resurrection. The resurrection of the Christ was no ordinary feat; nothing like that has ever happened before in human history. Yes, people were raised from the dead before by prophets and by Jesus Himself and by His apostles but not like this! They all died again, including Jesus' friend Lazarus (John 11:1-44). But not Jesus! His resurrection is different; He dies no more! death has no more dominion over Him. He conquered death for us all (Rom.6:9-10).

The bodily resurrection of Christ is the foundation event of His exaltation. All three persons of the Trinity participated in this event. Jesus, speaking as God asserted that He had the power to lay His life down and pick it up again, that He is the resurrection and the life (John 10:18,11:25). Referring to His own body he said, "Destroy this temple, and I will raise it again in three days" (John 2:19). A mere man cannot raise Himself from the dead, but one who is also God incarnate most certainly could and did.

But the resurrection is also the work of God the Father. The New Testament (NT) has frequently credited the resurrection as an act of God the Father. Peter in his sermon on the Day of Pentecost charged the religious leaders, his own countrymen, of doing a horrible thing, crucifying the Lord of Glory:

> Fellow Israelites, listen to this: Jesus of Nazareth was a man accredited by God to you by miracles, wonders and signs, which God did among you through him, as you yourselves know. This man was handed over to by God's deliberate plan and foreknowledge, and you, with the help of wicked men, put him death by nailing him cross. But God raised him from the dead, freeing him from the agony of death, because it was impossible for death to keep its hold on him. (Acts 2: 22-24).

Peter goes on to say, "God has raised this Jesus to life, and we are all witnesses of it. Exalted him to the right hand of God, he has received from the Father the promised Holy Spirit and has poured out what you now see and hear" (vv.32-33). There are numerous other passages of God the Father raising His Son from the dead which include these (Acts3:26, 5:30; 1Cor.6:14; Eph.1:20).

The resurrection was an act of the Triune God which means, the Holy Spirit also participated. The apostle Paul declares, "And if the Spirit of him who raised Jesus from the dead is living in you, he who raised Christ from the dead will also give life to your mortal bodies because of his Spirit who lives in you" (Rom.8:11).

Without the resurrection of the Christ, the redemption of humans would not be possible, and the establishment of the spiritual kingdom preached by Jesus would have been a failure. All these failures would have made God no less God, but all the claims of Jesus would have been left buried with Him and humans would have been forever doomed (John 3:16;1 Cor.15:12-19).

The resurrection of the Christ was not the resurrection of God, because God did not die, and God cannot die. The perfect sinless man, Jesus Christ died. He did not die under the weight of His own sins because He had none. The first Adam died under the weight of his own sins (Gen.3:1-7; Rom.5:12).

But Jesus Christ, the Second Adam, died under the weight of our sins. "[For] God made him who had no sin to be sin for us, so that in him we might become the righteousness of God" (2 Cor. 5:21). Christ did not die for Himself; He died vicariously for us. His death was an atonement, ransom, a substitutionary sacrifice offered unto God (Isa. 53:4-12 KJV; Rom.5:1-8). Jesus died to save humans from their sin and to restore what the first Adam loss by sin and death in the Fall (Matt.1:21; 1Cor.15:12; Rom.5:1-5).

Jesus Christ succeeded because He came back to life through the transforming power of the resurrection. And that coming back is unique and unparallel because no one has every returned like that before. For that reason, Jesus is called, "the firstborn from among the dead," and "the firstfruits of them that slept" (1Cor.15: 20-23). He came back with more than he had before He died. He came back not just as one resuscitated but overflowing with life and added capabilities. He left no decaying parts in the grave and

He dies no more; death has no more dominion over Him. Death is beaten, conquered, and will be completely done away with as the last enemy of the human family (1Cor.15: 51-56).

The resurrection body of the Christ was identified as the person who lived, who died, and is now back to life again (John 20:17-29). He claimed to be the same person (Rev.1:17-18).

He was the same person, yet there are differences. Though recognized as the same person, and His body bears the marks of His passion, at times He was not recognized, He could vanish at will, and even walked through closed doors or walls (John 20:19-23, 26-27). His resurrection body dies no more (Rom.6:9-10; Heb.10:12). No person previously raised from the dead or after has ever displayed these unique qualities. For these reasons, the resurrection of the Christ is in a category all to itself; it is classified as the *firstfruits* of them that slept (1Cor.15:20-23).

The implication of Firstfruits is that the greater harvest of its kind will follow. At His coming all believers will be resurrected and given a body like Jesus' (1 John 3:1-2). The resurrection of the Christ is the first event in the exaltation process of the Christ. Because of His resurrection, His prior glory is restored in answer to His high priestly prayed (John 17:1-5; Rev. 1: 9-18). Without the resurrection the ascension would not have taken place.

The Ascension of the Christ

The ascension of the Christ is the second major event in the exaltation of the Christ. But what is the ascension? The ascension is Jesus going from one place to another in the universe, from earth to heaven (Act 1:9-11). The implication is that heaven is a place as earth is a place (John 14: 1-4; Acts 7:55-56; Rev.4:1-4).

But the ascension has other significations; it is much more than the Christ being taken from one place to another. First, it signifies, mission accomplished, that Jesus Christ has victoriously walked through three set of gates: the gate of birth, the gates of death and hell, and now the gates of heaven (Ps.24:7-10; Eph.4:7-10). When an earthly monarch receives his or her throne, we refer to it as his or her ascension to the throne.

Second, the ascension is the indication that the resurrected Christ is His fully restored to His preincarnate position and glory (John17:1-5; Rev.1:10-18).

Third, He ascended to heaven not just as God, but as perfect man to assume new positions, honors, dignity, functions, and titles conferred upon Him by the Father.

Fourth, never before has the status of God-Man being given to human or any being in the heavenly community. In this God-Man union, perfect God and perfect Man are permanently joined in one body. As God He retains His title as KING over the Universe and as the perfect Man receives the honors and titles conferred upon Him by the Father.

The Session at the Father's Right Hand

The Mediatorial position at the Father's right hand is third in the state of exaltation of the Christ. Christ at the right hand of the Father is a literal and symbolic position (Acts 7:54-56). Literal in the sense that in ancient times, the person who sat at the king's right hand was the most loyal and most trusted in that administration. It is a position of honor, power, and authority.

In time the literal faded and the symbolic became dominant. Joseph to the Pharoah of Egypt, Daniel to the Kings of Babylon under whom he served, Nehemiah to Cyrus were so trusted, you could say, they were the kings right hand men. Today the term, this is my right-hand man is commonly used in all levels of business relationships.

First, Christ is exalted to highest place of honor and all created beings in the universe, including the communities of humans and angels, are commanded to submit to His authority and worship Him as they do the Father (Philip.2:9-11; Heb.1:1-9). This position of authority includes Kingdom's administration and leadership. Jesus Himself informs us that authority is given unto Him in heaven and on earth (Matt.28:18-20).

Second, Jesus Christ is exalted to the position of High Priest. This is a position in which at least two created beings have failed, one in heaven, the other on earth: Lucifer and Adam.

A High Priest is not only a worship leader; he oversees worship leaders or priests. Because worship is so important to God, we consider worship the food of God. Lucifer, an archangel in rank, is believed to have been head over all that pertains to worship.

Perhaps he was created for this very purpose of worship leading, according to scriptural implications. If worship is the food of God, Lucifer was the head chef; he was very close to God. From this vantage point, Lucifer thought he could be in the number one position and become the object of worship. He led a revolt to secure the position for himself and failed (Isa.14; Ezek.28; Rev.12).

Adam, the man of earth, God's man was also extremely close to God, and undoubtedly the guardian of worship. He and his wife were covered with divine glory. They had fellowship with God until the protocol of worship was breached with the help of Lucifer in the Paradise Garden. As Lucifer got thrown out of heaven, the man and his wife got thrown out of Paradise.

In Jesus Christ, paradise lost has become paradise regained for humans. Paul, the apostle writes, "Therefore, if any man be in Christ, he is a new creation" (2 Cor.5:17). The God-Man has enjoined the perfect man and the perfect God in one person, and is now occupying the place of High Priest, worship leader in heaven. And on earth, the blessed Holy Spirit is the true worship leader; He supervises acceptable worship and hands it off to the High Priest in the heavenly sanctuary (John 4:21-24; Acts 2:21-4, 38-39).

Third, in His mediator position, Jesus Christ functions as judge and advocate (see Vol.2). This judicial function is not only over the church but over the world. On earth God has given the sword of justice to civil government (Gen.9; Rom.7). But if wickedness gets out of control, God steps in to control it. God gives authority of discipline to the church. Where the church fails to exercise it, the Lord of the Church steps in (1Cor.11; Rev.2-3). Jesus Christ is the believers' defense attorney (advocate 1John 2:1-2) when the believer is accused by Satan (see Vol.2).

Scholars refer to the right-hand position as the session at the Father's right-hand because it ends with the second advent.

The Christ Who Returns to Reign

Some scholars exclude the return of Christ to reign from His state of exaltation, but that is a giant mistake. Jesus Christ returns to earth as KING of Kings and LORD of Lords; that is the summit of His exaltation (Rev.19). This is the time the whole world will visibly see the Christ in command and wearing the King's crown of leadership (Rev.19:16).

Jesus did not wear a king's crown at His first advent, and He did not ascend to heaven wearing a king's crown, and He was never envisioned wearing a king's crown in heaven by Stephen, Paul, or John except this time returning to earth. Therefore, the crowing must have taken place in heaven before He returns to earth to put down His enemies and to reign over the earth as this book suggests.

This book is primarily about His coronation of the Christ and the marriage supper celebration. These are the grand finale of the heavenly activities before Christ and His Church return to earth to rule, accompanied with an army of angels. To exclude this from His exaltation is like ending Handel's Messiah without singing the Halleluiah Chorus. For in a literal sense indeed, the kingdoms of this world have become the Kingdom of our God and of His Christ.

Summary

The exaltation of the Christ as we have seen is complex and includes many events and functions, some have been revealed but some are still classified. The full glory of the Christ is not going to be unveiled until we get there to behold it (John 17:24). Perhaps that's what Paul is implying when he said, "Eye has not seen, nor ear heard, nor have entered the heart of man the things which God has prepared for those who love Him"(1Cor.2:9 NKJV).

Bear in mind the four major themes covered in the exaltation of the Christ: His resurrection, His ascension, His position at the Father's righthand, and His return to reign. There are also significant subthemes, all of which are not named here. But they include His High Priestly functions, His function as advocate and judge, and events such as the marriage of the Lamb, and the marriage supper celebration. All these and more constitute the exaltation of the Christ.

The coronation of the Christ takes place within this context. I regard it is the grand finale culminating with the marriage supper celebration banquet followed by the return to earth to reign. With these events in mind, we now look at the coronation of the Christ more closely in the next chapter.

CHAPTER 5

THE CORONATION OF THE CHRIST

♛

Overview

In His first advent Jesus Christ refused to be crowned King against His assigned mission and against the will and purpose of His Father. His mission was not to restore the Davidic kingdom to Israel at that time, but to redemptively establish the kingdom of God; this is the spiritual rule of God in the hearts of humankind.

The spiritual kingdom is the invisible aspect of the His visible universal kingdom; it is the kingdom of God in you. God could not rule over territorial Israel until He rules in the heart of its people. That is why the law of the New Covenant is written not on tables of stone, but inwardly on the hearts of God's people. Jesus came to redemptively win people to God inwardly; that is the only way humans can be ruled, spiritually from within.

For this reason, Jesus refused to restore the visible, provincial, and territorial Davidic kingdom to Israel at His first coming. It would require the overthrow of Rome thus making Him a small time, political revolutionary like Barabbas. This limited territorial kingdom rule was against His mission, and against His Father's will and purpose. That refusal made Him the enemy of Israel's religious elite and resulted in His crucifixion.

But like Joseph (Jacob's son), the very thing his brothers meant for evil, God used it to save their lives and the whole nation of Egypt from starvation and death due to famine. God is using the malicious death of Jesus Christ to accomplish His perfect will and purpose, redemptively. Having accomplished His mission, God the Father has highly exalted Him.

The coronation of the Christ is part of that exaltation process as shown in Chapter 4. But we must also bear in mind that the ascension terminates in heaven a welcome back celebration as the conquering King of glory offered by the heavenly community (Psalm 24:7-9). In this chapter we will answer four main questions: what is the coronation? Who is being crowned? When and where is the coronation? And why the coronation?

Coronation Viewed Ordinarily

Coronation from an ordinary human perspective is the act of placing or bestowing a crown upon the head of a person who would become king or queen. It refers not only to the physical crowning but to the whole investiture ceremony, the robing, the presentation of regalia, scepter, and other items that are symbols of the monarch's dignity, authority, and power.

Additionally, a coronation most often includes an act of consecration and blessing in which a spiritual authority provides the invocation prayer and blessing, direct the taking of vows, and anointing the subject with holy oil. In some cases, "The monarch's consort may also be crowned, either simultaneously with the monarch or at a separate event." With that in mind, we turn our attention to a more superior coronation.

The Coronation of the Christ

The coronation of the Christ is no ordinary event. It is most unique and unparallel; it has no equal in the Universe. It is the investiture ceremony in which the risen, ascended, and exalted Christ is crowned KING of Kings and LORD of Lord by both communities, heaven and earth. The coronation is the continuation of His exaltation and majestic glorification as the God-Man to the highest place of honor, power, dignity, and authority in all of creation (Philip.2: 9-11). The term "God-Man" means that the Christ is truly Man (human) and truly God; all the fullness of God dwells in Him bodily (Col.1:19-20).

The coronation of the Christ must be viewed against the background of the Old Testament revelation of God as the King who reigns, not just over Israel, but over the universe as shown in chapter 1. The coronation must also be understood in the New Testament (NT) context of the exaltation of the Christ as already explained in chapter 4.

The coronation investiture ceremony appears to have a three-fold participation: (1) God the Father is the One doing exalting, the presentation, and the crowning of His Son. This is fitting because the Father is the One who the appointed His Son the highest of position and honor, and only God can crown God (Acts 17:31; Philip.2:9-11).

(2) Since the God-Man is the only Being crowned KING of Kings and LORD of Lords, it is also fitting that redeemed humans over whom He exercises rule participate in His coronation. Such participation signifies three very important things:

- First, it demonstrates that those who are being ruled over are free moral agents who in love pledge loyalty to Christ the King. It further implies that the Kingship of the Christ is not being forced upon us. He created us in love, and He redeemed us in love, and we responded in love. Unlike the antichrist government, Jesus does not force worship; it is given freely given out of love and loyalty. It is the nature of the new covenant to operate from the inner sanctum of the human heart (Jer.31:31-34).

- Second, it signifies that we redeemed humans share in the divinity of the God-Man as He shares our humanity. He is not just like us; He is one with us (Heb.2:10-11). We were created and recreated in God's image and likeness (2Cor. 5:17). We are God's children; we are heirs and co-heirs with Jesus Christ. We share in His glory and in the Father's inheritance (Rom.8 14-17; 1John 3:1-3).

- Third, it is fitting that we as redeemed humans participate in the coronation of the Christ, because it is one of the chief reasons for this general assembly gathering and celebration in heaven (Heb.12:22-24). We were invited and summoned by a trumpet blast to come for it is time and all is ready (Rev.19: 9; 1Thess.4:1618).

(3) The third and final group of beings that appear to participate in the coronation of the Christ are angels of varying ranks over whom the Christ exercises rule. There is no directly stated scriptural proof of this, but the implications are overwhelming. The Son of God is superior to all angels, and the angels serve the Son (Philip.2:9-1; Heb.1-2).

Angels are to heaven what humans are to earth; they are God's agents. The administration of the Christ is fraught with the ministry of angels, and especially activities from the rapture through the Great Tribulation, the marriage supper celebrations to the *Second Advent,* angels of varying ranks are very busy (Rev.4-19). Humans have a uniquely different relationship to God from angels; we are family angels are servants (Heb. 1:14).

Who Is Being Crowned?

It is self-evident the God-Man, Jesus Christ, is being crowned; let's explore that a little closer in this section. Jesus Christ is the only Being in the universe and in the administration of God Almighty who is truly God and truly Man. He is the person Bible scholars and theologians refer to as the God-Man. He is crowned by heaven and earth as KING of Kings and LORD of Lords (Rev.19:16).

Beyond the fact that this is no ordinary position; it is a profound mystery that no mere mortal can fully comprehend. Beginning with the incarnation, God and perfect man became united as one person and is now eternally made permanent in that form (Col.1:15-20). Who in the Universe is qualified to preside over such event? The answer to the question is—God the Father alone determines the time, the place, and the process leading to the coronation of His Son, not just as King over Israel, but as KING of Kings and LORD of Lords over the Universe in general and the earth in particular.

But that is not all. The God side of the God-Man equation was always KING of the Universe. Where the proverbial tire meets the road is the Man side of this coronation mystery—the Man is crowned KING and LORD not just over Israel and the whole earth, geographically, but over the spiritual kingdom redemptively established in the hearts of humankind. The mission of the first advent of the Christ was to make this invisible, internal kingdom in the hearts of humans possible. Humans must be won inwardly; they cannot be ruled by brute force externally. They were uniquely wired by the Lord Himself at creation as free moral agents, and redemption preserves that freedom (Gen.1: 26-28; John 8:36; Gal.5:1).

Where And When Is the Coronation?

We will consider four scenarios concerning the place and time of the coronation of the Christ. *First, the coronation of the Christ will be in heaven.* This fact is supported scripturally and logically. Heaven is the place Jesus said he was returning to prepare a place for us and would bring us there (John 14: 1-3). Heaven is where Christ bodily resides since His ascension (Acts 1:9-11). Stephen being stoned to death for the sake of the gospel saw Jesus in heaven (Acts 7: 54-60).

The coronation and the events surrounding it are depicted as taking place in heaven, sometime after the rapture, and after the believers' judgment, and perhaps after the marriage of the Lamb, but most certainly before the marriage supper celebration (Rev.19:1-10).

Second, both Old and New Testaments saints will be present at the coronation of the Christ. Some scholars are of the notion that Old Testament (OT) saints will not be resurrected with New Testament (NT) saints to be together in heaven for the coronation and the marriage supper, so for Israel's sake such events will be on earth. That doctrine is not only a stretch but appears to be false.

The truth is both Old and New Testaments saints have been redeemed by the sacrifice of Jesus Christ on the cross and all will be resurrected to attend these events in heaven (1Thes.4:16-17; John 5:28-29; 1Cor.15:51-54). In Christ there is no distinction of

Gentiles or Jews; we are all member of one Body. The notion that OT believers and NT believers will be resurrected at different times is theological invention, designed to maintain doctrinal consistency on the part of those holding a particular eschatological view, namely ultra-dispensationalism.

Again, believers of both Testaments are redeemed by Christ's sacrificial work on the cross and bear no particular Jew or Gentile distinction in Christ in this sense (Isa.53; John 10:14-16; Eph.2:11-20). National Israel will receive the Messiah at His Second Advent and will be given accommodations that are now partly classified but will be fully revealed then. Perhaps, there will be some celebration after Christ rescues Israel, triumphs at Armageddon or upon or after His ascension to the throne of king David in Jerusalem (Isa. 9: 6-7).

Third, *Jesus Christ requested of His Father that His people come where He is to behold His glory* (John 17:24). Just as the Queen of Sheba had to leave her place to go to Israel to behold Solomon's glory, so we must leave the earth realm to see the glory of Jesus. Jesus Christ further informs us that He was going ahead to make accommodation (John 14:1-4). Blessed are they that are invited to the Marriage Supper of the Lamb. It is an invitation to the whole investiture ceremony, coronation, and celebration.

Fourth, since all believers will already be in heaven for the believers' judgment and rewards (2 Cor.5:10), by extension they will be there for the coronation and marriage supper celebration, according to the biblical record (Rev.19:1-8). People out of every nation, race, language, and ethnicity will be present there.

The Coronation of God's People

Believers will not only participate in the coronation of the Christ, but many will also be crowned and honored with various titles; prominent among these are Kings and Lords.

Kings and Lords are presumably, the two highest leadership titles to be conferred. The Christ is crowned KINGS of Kings and LORD of Lords (Rev.19:16). The implication is that He will be ruling over Kings and Lords among and other titles.

Under ordinary human coronation in the beginning section of this chapter, it is stated that *consorts* of a monarch are at times crowned on or about the same time the monarch is crowned. This appears to be true in the coronation of the Christ. Since the Church is considered the Bride of Christ and by extension the Queen because the Groom is the KING of Kings, it is not unrealistic that the bride would also be crowned.

There is stronger scriptural evidence that some believers will be awarded crowns in connection with the believers' judgment (see Vol.2). Crowns are symbols of honor and leadership; they symbolize the highest level of leadership.

Furthermore, Jesus Christ is not returning to earth alone or to rule alone. He departs the portals of heaven with many crowns on His head, riding under the title KING of Kings and LORD of Lords and is followed by a vast multitude of saints and angels (Rev.19: 18-16). He is heading for earth to put down the illegitimate rulers and establish His Kingdom with His people.

The Crown Accepted

In chapter 3 of this book, Jesus rejected being taken by force and crowned king by political zealots and religious enthusiasts during His first advent. He refused to being bribed into kingship by Satan or pressured by His own disciples to restore the kingdom to Israel at that time against His Father's will and purpose. His strong sense of mission would not allow Him to do that.

But now at the coronation in heaven, the Lord Jesus proudly accepts the crown and titles of KING of Kings and LORD of Lords. Why? The answer to this question has already been given in several ways, and at the risk of being redundant, the answers need to be restated briefly and clearly.

First, Jesus refused to be crowned king during His first advent because He was already King over the Universe He created. To become incarnate, He divested Himself of the glory and majesty that come with that *Universal Kingdom*, but He did not relinquish the title of King or denied that He was (John 18:33-36).

Second, Jesus refused to be crowned king during His first advent, because it was against His mission and against His Father's purpose to restore the Davidic kingdom to Israel at that time, even though the religious elite, the common people, and His own little group of disciples pressured Him to do it.

Third, to accept being crowned king over Israel by force or willingly would have been a poor compromise. He would be king over one little nation by leading a Barabbas style political revolution against Rome.

Fourth, to accept being crowned king during His first advent would mean sidestepping the cross and by extension the redemption of humankind; no cross, no atonement for sin.

Fifth, any compromise to become king at the time of His first advent would be the inevitable acceptance of Satan's offer to make Him king over the kingdoms of this world with the glory of them (Matt.4:8-10).

Finally, had Jesus chosen to be crowned King during His first advent, He would have had to forego the inauguration of the spiritual kingdom of God that was the theme of His ministry's preaching and teaching. Humans cannot be won to God unless they are won inwardly. The spiritual kingdom deals with the inner sanctum; it is the rule of God established in the hearts of humans. That is what Jesus means when He said, "the kingdom of God is in you" (Luke 17:21). Surrendering His life on the cross for the salvation of humans was the Father's will for His Son, but it was not forced upon Him. Jesus voluntarily chose that path. He made it clear that no man takes his life from him, that he has power to lay down his life and take it up again (John 10:18).

Gethsemane settled the matter between the human and divine will; there Jesus voluntarily submitted His human will to the divine will when He said to the Father, "Not my will but thine be done (Matt.26:39-42). This struggle between the human and the Divine will should not be underestimated; it was a real battle fought and won that night on His face in agonizing prayer against the prince of darkness. Mel Gibson's Passion of the Christ got it right, showing the snake sliding behind the praying Jesus, then the shadowy figure of Satan behind Him while the disciples slept.

All true believers will face a similar struggle; the apostle Paul speaks of his struggle and how he won the victory through Jesus Christ (Rom.7:14-25).

Jesus' prayer down on His face in Gethsemane is, perhaps, the secret to the successful, triumphant mission of His first advent. But of course, the created universe held its collective breaths from the moment He breathed His last on that cross until resurrection morning. It's like the radio silence Huston's control center experience when the Apollo was on the dark side of the moon. The dead silence of the control center erupted in jubilation when it was broken with one word, Huston!

When He was upon earth, Satan offered to make Him king over the kingdoms of this world in their splendor (Matt.4:8-11). Jesus rejected the offer because it was presumptuous and illegitimate; it was against His mission and against His Father's will and purpose (Matt.26:39-42). Plus, He would have had to side-step the cross and the work of redemption.

Now, because of cross, billions of sons and daughters born into God's Kingdom and are now assembled in Heaven's Grand-Ballroom with the Father, angels, and archangels to crown Him KING of Kings and LORD of Lords.

PART III
THE MARRIAGE SUPPER

CORONATION OF THE CHRIST & THE MARRIAGE SUPPER

CHAPTER 6

THE MARRIAGE SUPPER CELEBRATION

The Marriage of the Lamb

The marriage of the Lamb precedes the *Marriage Supper* as a wedding ceremony precedes the reception; the same appears to be true here, and this chapter speaks of both events.

They are real heavenly events with no earthly parallel in terms of signification, scope, and grandeur. This is the place, and these are the events that every human with the gift of life should strive to be. But to get here is not so much what you know; it is who you know. If you know Jesus in a saving relationship, and He knows you, that is all the invitation you will ever need. You will be given a trumpet call when everything is ready.

The term marriage is used figuratively to illustrate Christ's union with His people. Marriage is a natural and spiritual relationship between a man and a woman; it is the closest and most joyful relationship on earth, so it is used figuratively to express a union that is other worldly or heavenly. There are at least two reasons the figure of marriage is used for this illustrative purpose. They are as follows:

(1) From the beginning of human history in the *Paradise Garden*, biblical marriage has been a human and divine relationship, a judicial transaction, a covenant between a man and a woman, a strong party and a weak one. Strong is not used here to mean physical or constitutional but positional.

The woman is the one who is uprooted from her family, her father's protection, and the resources of her father's house to enjoin herself to a stranger and his family. She is most vulnerable for abuse. In this sense, she is the weaker party. In like manner, God's relationship with His people is a legally binding covenant; He is the Almighty, the stronger party; they are the weaker ones.

This language of marriage is frequently used figurative in the Old Testament to illustrate the relationship between God and His covenant people, Israel (Isa. 54:1-7,62:4-5; Hos.2:16-20).[1]

(2) On earth, marriage is the most intimate and most joyous union two people can experience together. Earth has no other experience to illustrate a heavenly union besides marriage. For these reasons (1 & 2) the language of marriage is also used in the

THE MARRIAGE SUPPER CELEBRATION

New Testament to illustrate the union between Christ and His Church, an inseparable union (Eph.5: 21-33; Rom.8:35-39).

Even though the teaching of the preceding Ephesians passage is applicable to marriage, it is not primarily about marriage; it is about the love relationship between Christ and His Church. This truth is stated in these words, "For this reason a man will leave his father and mother and be united to his wife, and the two will become one flesh. This is a profound mystery—but I am talking about Christ and the church" (vv.31-32).

Once again, the language of marriage is deployed to illustrate the consummation of the permanent, indissoluble union between Jesus Christ and His people in the celebrations called, the *Marriage of the Lamb* and the *Marriage Supper* (Rom. 8:31-39; Rev.19: 6-8). Why?

Earth has no closer, joyous intimacy or language to illustrate the heavenly union between Christ and His people. The people of earth understand marriage; there is no better experience to use to help humans understand what will take place in heaven relationally. It is for that reason, among others, Jesus kept using the expression, "the kingdom of heaven is like." He used stores familiar to His hearers to explain something totally unfamiliar; marriage is use in a similar way, figuratively.

Heaven is not about marriage. Jesus Himself said, in heaven people will not be marrying or giving to marriage (Matt.22:23-33). Marriage is the best earth has to offer, so it is used to illustrate something heavenly that we have never experienced before. A royal wedding is perhaps the most fascinating thing earth has ever seen; we can relate to marriage or weddings.

Furthermore, note that a marriage always calls for an officiating third party who also bears witness. The officiating third party at the marriage-like union of the Lamb is God the Father, and the blessed Holy Spirit. But there is also a vast company of human participants who constitute the bride, and a great multitude of angels of various ranks as guests that bear witness as well (Heb.12:1-3; Rev.19:6-8). This is the same multitude of saints and angels that later accompany the KING back to earth in His second advent revelation to the world (Rev.19:11-16).

Angels are playing a significant role in the celebration because they have been in the service of God and humankind from creation until now. All heaven is participating in this magnificent family union. And rightly so for all created beings must confess the Lordship of the Christ and bend their knees in worship and adoration of Him (Phillp.2:9-11; Heb.1: 5-8).

God does nothing without significance. Just as God officiated in the first marriage ceremony of His son Adam to Eve, He now presides over this marriage-like union of His only begotten Son with His people. Human Marriage, among other purposes, was intended to point to this perfect union.

It is also fitting that the God-Man is now crowned by His people, and the crown is accepted because it is legitimately given. It was rejected before when offered upon earth by Satan and those who wanted to crown Him King by force for their own purpose. The crown was rejected at that time because it was illegitimately offered outside the Father's will and purpose.

The Wedding Supper Celebration

The wedding supper celebration is what we call a banquet; it comes after what is figuratively referred to as *the Marriage of the Lamb*, discussed in the previous section. This celebration undoubtedly falls in the context of the *Coronation* and the *Marriage* and *Marriage Supper of the Lamb*.

There are those who assert that the marriage supper will be held on earth to accommodate national Israel, but that seems to be a stretch. The scriptural text and context show these events taking place in heaven where a massive crowd of every nation, language, race, and tribe is already gathered (Rev.19:1-8).

Nation Israel will not embrace Jesus as their Messiah until after this, upon His return to earth. The Church began with Jews and throughout the Church age millions of them embraced Jesus as the Christ; they will be well represented at these events in heaven. As shown later, the Marriage Supper is a communion service consummating the union between Christ and His people; this is the first celebration of His passion as implied at the Last Supper on earth (Matt.26:28-29).

Also, the idea that OT saints will not be resurrected with NT saints to attend these events in heaven is another stretch of the Scriptures. Both Old and New Testament saints are redeemed by the sacrifice of Jesus on the cross (Heb. 9:11-10:15). Jesus Himself said, "there will be one-fold and one Shepherd (John 10:16).

Furthermore, the wedding supper appears to be the last major event in heaven before Christ and His people return to earth; that is, the second advent of the Christ (Rev.19:6-14).

On earth, when people get married, it is followed with a grand celebration. There is no reason to believe it will be otherwise in heaven. Except, the heavenly events will be indescribable in terms of grandeur. The coronation of the queen or king of England, a royal wedding, or the ascension of a Pope to the throne of Saint Peter's are the three most glorious and sacred pageantry that earth has conducted to date. But the coronation of the Christ, the Marriage and Marriage Supper of the Lamb will by far supersede these three earthly events combined.

No individual, family, government, or nation on earth has the resources to throw a party to compete with heaven. Heaven's celebration is sponsored by the God of the Universe, and He has been in planning for it a long time. These events will bring heaven and earth together, perhaps, for the grandest celebration of time and eternity and you are there. Or will you?

If you have a salvation relationship with Jesus Christ, you have an invitation and you will be there. It is the same invitation you accepted when you received Jesus Christ as the Savior and Lord of your life (John 3:16). "Blessed [happy] are those who are invited to the wedding supper of the Lamb" (Rev.19: 9). The wedding supper crowd is this same crowd that will return with Jesus Christ to earth to reign (Rev.19: 11-16, 20:6).

An Inscrutable Connection

There appears to be a connection between the Lord's Supper, instituted by Jesus and celebrated in churches throughout history and the Marriage Supper scheduled to be celebrated in heaven. The connection between these two suppers is missed or overlooked in the writings of many biblical scholars, so we will look at it the connection here (i.e., Last Supper--Marriage Supper).

During the week of His passion, a day or two before His crucifixion, Jesus celebrated His last Passover with His disciples; and at the same time, He instituted what we now call, the Lord's Supper. He made a statement while reclining at the table which appears to establish connection between His *Last Supper* on earth before His crucifixion and the *Marriage Supper of the Lamb* in heaven just before He returns to earth. Here is the statement:

> Then he took the cup, and when he had given thanks, he gave it to them saying, 'Drink from it all of you. This cup is my blood of the covenant, which is poured out for many for the forgiveness of sins. I tell you, I will not drink from this fruit of the vine from now on until that day when I drink it new with you in my Fathers kingdom.' (Matt.26:27-29)

The implication is that the *Marriage Supper* is the first true celebration the Lord Jesus is having with His people since that week of His crucifixion. After His resurrection, there are three occasions on record involving food, but none of these qualify as a celebration meal. In each, food was used as mere convenience to demonstrate something else to His disciples who were having difficulty accepting the reality of His bodily resurrection.

There are three examples:1) Jesus used food to reveal Himself (Luke 13-32). There is a way He conducted Himself at a table that was uniquely His, so even though He was in disguised, the way He broke the bread blew His cover. 2) Jesus used food to show that He was real and not a ghost (vv.36-44). For one, ghosts don't have substance that you can hold them and feel them and examine them for bodily marks. Ghost don't ask for food and consume it in your presence. Jesus did all that to prove he was not ghost but a real human being.

3) Jesus used food to restore a fallen disciple to ministry (John 21:10-15). One of the best icebreakers is food; the presence of food also helps to neutralize tension in a difficult situation and helps to restore relationships. That is the way food was used at this beach breakfast. It was no celebration meal in honor of His disciples or His disciples in honor of Him. It was no celebration meal such as that given honoring Jesus and Lazarus, after Lazarus came back to life in such a dramatic way (John 12:1-8).

That brings us back to the Lord's Supper statement of Jesus which appears to connect that supper to the *Marriage Supper of the Lamb*. If the connection is true, then the Marriage Supper is a massive *Lord's Supper* celebration of our redemption, a love feast at the family table in the presence of His Father and all of heaven.

The Marriage Supper is indeed Christ drinking of the fruit of the vine a new in His Father's Kingdom as He said. That makes this the mother of all joyful celebrations, uniting heaven, and earth as one family around the Father's table. We can all agree with Elisha A. Hoffman, "What a fellowship, what a joy divine, leaning on the everlasting arms...."

The Nature of the Marriage Supper Celebration

First, the Marriage Supper of the Lamb celebrates the redemptive union between Christ as His people. The word marriage illustrates that union, a union brought about by a better sacrifice and covenant of blood more precious than that of the old covenant. It was necessary, therefore, to wait until the overwhelming majority of the redeemed embraced that sacrifice and are gathered in once place to celebrate it.

This banquet celebration where the glorified, exalted Christ is bodily present as the centrally honored person, recalls the Last Supper He had on earth with His disciples during the week of His passion, in which He said He would not drink of the fruit of the vine again with them until it finds fulfillment in the Kingdom of God which was undoubtedly a reference to the Marriage Supper. From that hour the drama of His passion picked up speed.

He immediately rose from supper, laid aside His outer garment, pour water in a basin, and washed His disciples' feet. They then sang a hymn and went to the Garden of Gethsemane to pray. Gethsemane was a traumatic experience for our Lord.

While leaving the garden, Judas arrived with a group of soldiers; Jesus was arrested. Peter tried to defend Him, but Jesus objected. Most of the disciples fled but John and Peter followed to

Caiaphas' palace where Peter denied knowing Jesus. Everything went downhill from there. Jesus is shuttled from one hasty trial to another until he was finally handed over by the Roman governor for crucifixion. Everything was rushed, including the trials, the crucifixion, and burial because the Sabbath was at hand.

The crucifixion was most traumatic for everyone, so after His resurrection, Jesus had a forty-day debriefing of His disciples. This time of rest and healing was necessary. Jesus used that forty-day period to emotionally heal His disciples, including His mother and those women that closely supported His ministry. He also used the time to prepare them for the next stage of relationship and ministry without His physical, visible presence.

The forty days ended with the ascension, followed by Pentecost and active ministry. No vacation or celebration beyond the infant church breaking bread from house to house in their worship activities. Since they thought His return was most imminent, they urgently carried out the Great Commission.

The Marriage Supper of the Lamb is the first big, redemptive celebration gathering where Jesus is bodily and visible present with His people. It recalls the words of the poet, "then Lord hasten the day when faith shall be sight...." The Father will see His sons and daughters, and all heaven can celebrate around the Lord's table in a giant banquet supper.

Second, Marriage Supper is a victory celebration of joy and thankfulness. It is eucharistic, a giant holy communion.

Third, Marriage Supper is a diversified yet unified celebration with the people of God from every nation, race, and language united as one body in Christ, under the headship of one Lord.

The Marriage Supper is a gathering of both Jews and gentiles, in as much as nation Israel is absent. But let us not forget that the twelve apostles and much of the early church were Jewish, and all through church history, messianic Jews have entered the kingdom of God. Furthermore, this author believes that all the Old Testament saints will be there at the *Marriage Supper* because they too were redeemed by Christ's sacrifice on the cross.

A second insightful connection is found in another statement made by Jesus in the context of the Last Supper. After Supper Jesus said to His disciples, "You are those who have stood by me in my trials. And I confer on you a kingdom, just as my Father conferred one on me, so that you may eat and drink at my table in my kingdom and sit on thrones, judging the twelve tribes of Israel" (Luke 22 28-30).*The Marriage Supper* appears to be the fulfillment of this promise, note that after this supper, we will all return to earth to rule with the next section shows.

Finally, the *Married Supper* is an exalted, holy gathering, and it is by invitation only. Exalted because it is part of the exaltation of the Christ; the exaltation is a process of many events. It is holy and righteous as represented by the attire of the saints (fine lining, clean and white). And yes, it is by invitation only. The angel said to John, "Blessed [happy] are those who are invited to the Wedding Supper of the Lamb!" (Rev.19:9).

And Supper Being Ended

The Marriage Supper ends our rendezvous in heaven; this is perhaps our first and last use of this place called heaven. This is the old heaven; there is going to be a new one. God will be relocating. We have been here for about seven years since we were raptured by a trumpet blast (1Thess. 4:16-18).

We had our court appearance here at the *Believers' Judgment* (2 Cor.5:10). We attended rewards ceremonies, coronation ceremony, we attended what is figuratively called, the *Marriage of the Lamb*, and finally the Marriage Supper celebration banquet (Rev.19:6-8). And what a glorious time we have had but the party has ended but not heaven, for wherever Jesus is, is heaven for us.

It is on the schedule for Jesus to return to earth, and the KING has gotten an urgent call back to earth and we must accompany Him. After the earthly Lord's Supper, Jesus poured water into a basin and washed His disciples' feet. But in heaven, no sooner than the Marriage Supper is ended, duty calls again, and we must return to earth, urgently. Some will ask, but why?

The next chapter will give you a clearer and fuller answer to the question. But I will say this much, on earth a massive Satanic deception has run its course, doing great harm to God's covenant people Israel, and once again Jesus must lead the rescue mission, and we are with Him!

CHAPTER 7

THE WARRIOR KING RETURNS TO REIGN

While the people of God taken from the earth during the rapture are celebrating in heaven, the fire of the *Great Tribulation* has intensified tremendously on earth. Nature has turned against humankind in frightening cosmic calamities: the planetary heaven, the seas, the rivers of water, the earth have all turned against wicked humankind. There is famine, war, and diseases. To add insult to injury, personified evil has taken control of government; to be frank, Satan is fully in charge.

The global dictator (the Antichrist) and his sidekick, the False prophet, with their military war machine are tightening the noose of annihilation around Israel's neck. Satan acting through certain

Gentile nation States, has long been bent on destroying the State of Israel and its people. This is Satan's ideal opportunity to pull it off, but it will not accomplish its desired end; it's a divine setup to destroy the enemies of Israel.

Individual Jews have embraced Jesus as their messiah throughout the history of the Church; in our time, we call them messianic Jews. But from the *First Century* A.D. national Israel rejected the true messiah, Jesus Christ. He came to them in His Father's name, and they had Him crucified (John 1:12).

At that time Jesus told them, "I have come in my Father's name, and you do not accept me; but if someone else comes in his own name, you will accept him" (John 5:43). That prophecy has now come to fruition and Israel has accepted a false Messiah.

Despite having the written revelation of God, Israel rejected the true Messiah when He arrived among them. The apostle Paul said, "For this cause, God shall send them strong delusion, that they should believe a lie: that they all might be damned who believe not the truth but have pleasure in unrighteousness" (2 Thess.2: 11-12 KJV). The Antichrist is that deceiver who comes in his own name and Israel accepts him (Rev.13:1-10).

Israel not only accepts this deceiver as their Messiah, but they also signed a covenant (treaty) with him. This treaty with Israel is signed at the beginning of the seven years of *Great Tribulation*, when the Antichrist first appears on the scene. Israel will be given favored nation status, such as they now enjoy with the United States. They are guaranteed economic, and military security.

But the Antichrist has no intension of abiding by this treaty; it is a Satanic deception; three and a half years later, the treaty will be broken (Dan.9:20-27). Israel will be left with no friends, no security, and extremely vulnerable in a sea of enemies.

The United States is not reflected in the prophetic happenings at this time, scholars believe she must have ceased to be a viable economic and military power. And that could explain why Israel needs to look elsewhere for her security needs. The Antichrist's protection would be the only alternative for Israel.

As noted earlier, forty-two months after the agreement with Israel, the antichrist would have consolidated his global power and can now reveal his true satanic character. The treaty was a deception from the beginning to control the Jews and Israel to serve Satan's purpose. Israel is now at the mercy of her enemies whose purpose is to utter destroy her.

In as much as Israel is a secular State, the principles of the Torah shape and guide its policies and national values. They will not knowingly worship Satan or any human proxy for Satan. The Antichrist knows this and cleverly camouflages its satanic intent.

At the treaty's signing, Israel had no idea that this Beast will demand worship of all people groups (Rev.13:11-17). Or, if known, Israel is granted exemption from the *Mark of the Beast and worship of its image.* Persons who take this biometric mark belong to Satan and must worship the Antichrist who is Satan's proxy. The Antichrist knows that the Torah forbids such and no true Jews would sign document committing themselves to such idolatry and blasphemy. But now the Antichrist is strong; he can ignore the terms of the treaty and use his military machine to enforce compliance with his policies which are economic and religious.

Furthermore, the Antichrist knows that since the holocaust, Jews are verry skittish about taking bodily identification marks. For these reasons the treaty includes exemption clause to the *Mark of the Beast,* if this ID is already required. It sweetens the deal for the Jews to sign the deceptive treaty. But God has a strong hand in the matter, for those who take the Mark of the Beast are permanently Satan's. God will not allow Israel to take the mark for they are His covenant people and will abide by His Word in this case.

With the treaty broken, the Antichrist now enforces his global policy of worship on all nations, peoples, and languages (Rev.13:11-18). Israel with Torah in hand will worship no other God but Yahweh and that puts the nation on a collision course with the Antichrist's military machine.

Israel is left friendless and helpless as a coalition of nations with combined nuclear arsenal besieged Jerusalem and all Israel, to annihilate her off the face of the earth. Satan wanted to do this a long time ago but could not find any human agent to work through until now. What Egypt, Assyria, Babylon, Persia, Rome, and Hitler's Germany could not do, now looks like an achievable mission. Like a little lamb surrounded by a thousand wolves is Israel.

Israel has only one card left to play and that is to look upward and call on the God of Abraham, Isaac, and Jacob for help, and that is exactly what she does. The cry for help is urgent and the response from heaven is swift and immediate. The cry comes up to heaven just as we are ending the Marriage Supper of the Lamb. Jesus rises from supper not to pour water in a basin and wash anyone's feet as He did at the Last Supper on earth, but to signal His departure to earth will all heaven following Him.

The Warrior King Returns

With an army of saints and angels following, Jesus exits the portals of heaven riding a war horse, a milk white stallion, not a meek and quiet donkey as when He entered Jerusalem on what we call Palm Sunday. His destination is earth, the country Israel, the city, Jerusalem. The apostle John describes the scene for us:

> I saw heaven standing open and there before me was a white horse, whose rider is called Faithful and True. With justice he judges and wages war. His eyes are like blazing fire, and on his head are many crowns. He has a name written on him that no one knows but he himself. He is dressed in a robe dipped in blood, and his name is the Word of God. The armies of heaven were following him, riding on white horses and dressed in fine linen, white and clean. Coming out of his mouth is a sharp sword with which to strike down the nations. He will rule with an iron scepter. He treads the winepress of the fury of the wrath of God Almighty. On his robe and his thigh, he has this name: KING of Kings and LORD of Lords. (Rev.19:11-16)

When you read the preceding scripture passage, you see the KING leading His army into battle, but He is the only one doing the fighting. He is bent on justice and judgment and is determined to put down His enemies by Himself, and alone He did (Isa.63:1-6).

Israel is rescued from annihilation, they finally embraced Jesus as their true Messiah, the gentiles' war machines are destroyed, and millions of troops lay dead. Much of the story is yet to be unfolded; after the summary, you must now go to Volume 5 to continue the story.

Summary

We have been to His Majesty's dwelling place and the seat of His government, and we have seen and participated in events beyond our language to describe, and all this is just the beginning of things to come. We know at some point not only God's dwelling but His government, and the eternal capital will be relocating to earth, the new earth, and the new world order will be established.

So, we are not going to heaven on permanent vacation. In fact, as you have seen, it is a working vacation. We will return to earth to run a government with the KING of Kings, and LORD of Lords. Anywhere He is that's heaven for us. Our prayer is about to be fulfilled, "Thy kingdom come, thy will be done on earth as it is in heaven" (Matt.6:10).

The events covered in volumes I, II, III, and now IV deal with *Related Events to the Second Coming of the Christ*. Volume V deals with the true event, *The Second Coming of the Christ*. There are many events associated with His Second Coming that will unfold in the remaining volumes of the series.

END NOTES

Introduction

1. Dewar, Michael W. *The Believers Judgment & Rewards.* New York: Dwelling Place Cleansing, 2022.

Chapter 1

1. George Arthur Buttrick, Editor. *The Interpreter's Dictionary of the Bible.* Vol.3. New York: Abingdon Press, 1962. (pp.11-12).

2. Unger, Merrill F. Harrison, R.K. (Editor). *The New Unger's Bible Dictionary.* Chicago, IL: The Moody Bible Institute of Chicago, 1988, 781.

3. *The New Unger's Bible Dictionary*, Peace (Shalom). 980-981.

4. Ryre, Charles Caldwell. Study Bible (ESV). *Introduction to Judges.* Chicago, IL: Moody Bible Institute, 1986.

Chapter 3

1. Berkhof, Louis. *Systematic Theology: New Combined Edition*. Grand Rapids, MI: William B. Eerdmans Publishing Co. 1996.

2. Mark Oakley, Mark. *Palm Sunday Sermon*. Saint Patrick, London. https://www.youtube.com/watch?v=92DYZl7Y4n8

Chapter 4

1. See "Coronation" in Noah webster 1828 Dictionary

2. Berkhof, Louis. *Systematic Theology* (the exaltation of Christ)

Chapter 6

1. *The Interpreters Dictionary of the Bible* Vol.3 (K-Q), 284-285.

ABOUT THE AUTHOR

Michael W. Dewar, Sr. is a pastor, Bible teacher, and mentor in the spiritual life. He is a Licensed Master Social Worker, and a specialist in church and family conflicts. He trains Agents of Peace-Managers of Conflicts to launch peace ministries in local churches.

Reverend Dewar is the founder and pastor of New York Congregational Baptist Church (NYCBC), and the author of several books, including a three-volume training course on *Church and Family Conflicts*.

He holds earned degrees from several institutions of higher learning, including the Master of Divinity from what is now Palmer Theological Seminary, Eastern University, the MSW from Wurzweiler School of Social Work, Yeshiva University, the LMSW from the State of New York, and a doctorate from Regent University, School of Divinity.

Reverend Dewar lives in New York City with his family.

CORONATION OF THE CHRIST & THE MARRIAGE SUPPER

OTHER BOOKS BY THIS AUTHOR

First 3 of a 10 Volume series

CORONATION OF THE CHRIST & THE MARRIAGE SUPPER

Start a Peace Ministry in Your Church

Text Book

Instructor's Manual   Student's Manual

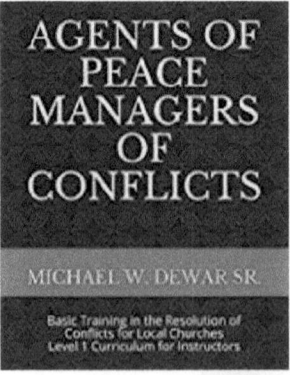   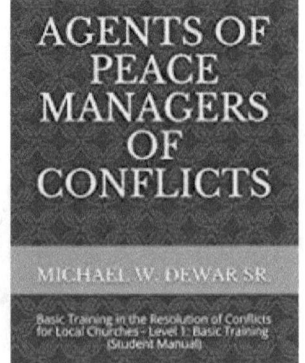

OTHER BOOKS BY THIS AUTHOR

Two Set of Books in Heaven; Your name is in One. Check to see and make necessary changes.

OTHER BOOKS BY THIS AUTHOR

www.ingramcontent.com/pod-product-compliance
Lightning Source LLC
Chambersburg PA
CBHW071712040426
42446CB00011B/2027